OZMER – DEVADER

The Ancestors of Donna Marie Higgins

Compiled and Edited by Stanton Darnbrook Colson

OZMER – DEVADER

The Ancestors of
Donna Marie Higgins

Compiled and Edited by
Stanton Darnbrook Colson

ISBN 13: 978-1506138763
ISBN 10: 1506138764

*Published by AAS White Heron Press
1623 Soundneck Road, Elizabeth City, NC 27909
White Heron Press and associated logos are trademarks
and/or
registered trademarks of American Artists' Studios*

Printed in the U.S.A.

Cover Design by Kim Colson

This Book
Chronicles the
Ozmer and Devader Families
Ancestors of Donna Marie Higgins

[Additional photographs, documents
and research for this book are on file
with Stanton Darnbrook Colson]

Please feel free to send any corrections,
changes and/or updates to the editor
at the email address provided below.

Stanton Darnbrook Colson
cwaveofobx@yahoo.com

Dedicated to
Anna Emma Devader

The Ozmer Family

Bernadine Marie Ozmer
and Robert Charles Higgins

The Life and Times of
Bernadine Marie Prudence Ozmer

PATERNAL ANCESTRY: [OZMER/OSMORE:
Windsor Wilkerson, Jefferson Gadwell, Robert Clark,
Richard, (William)]

MATERNAL ANCESTRY: [DEVADER/
DUIVETTER: Anna Emma[2], Peter[1] {of Belgium}
Jacobus-Frances[1a]]

BERNADINE MARIE was born
on November 4, 1925 at St. Marys,
Pottawatomie County, Kansas.
Her father was Windsor
Wilkerson "Jack" Ozmer of De-
Kalb County, Georgia and later of
St. Marys, Pottawatomie County,
Kansas. Her mother was Anna
Emma[2] Devader of Morris, Wyandotte County,
Kansas.

Bernadine Marie
Ozmer–10 Months

BERNADINE MARIE married Robert Charles[4]
Higgins on July 23, 1945 at Washington, D.C. The
ceremony was performed in St. Patrick's Catholic
Church by the Reverend James E. Cowhig. Robert[4]
was born on March 16, 1925 at Washington, D.C. He
died on February 19, 1982 of lung cancer at his home
on Antietam Drive, Fairfax, Fairfax County, Virginia.
His father was Joseph Francis[3] [John Joseph[2], John[1] {of

Ireland}] Higgins of Schenectady, Schenectady County, New York and later of Washington, D.C. and Alexandria, Virginia. His mother was Margaret Ellen [William Henry, Alvah, William, Joseph, Joseph {born circa 1723/1725 in Massachusetts}] Pitts of Castleton, Rensselaer County, New York.

BERNADINE MARIE, as a child, was acquainted with a woman by the name of Verdi Marstol in St. Marys, Kansas. Donna knew this was an important relationship for her mother because she had taken Donna and her sisters to visit Verdi while they were small children. Bernadine told Donna that Verdi and Gram [Bernadine's mother, Anna] were best friends and married around the same time, around World War I. When Gram's husband came home to see their infant son, he fell ill and died of the Spanish flu. Then on Friday, a week later, their baby died; then Friday a week afterwards, Verdi's husband died as well.

Both widows eventually remarried. Verdi had no children with her second husband but had a daughter from her first marriage. Gram had three children with "Jack." When they could not keep up with their rental house due to Jack's alcoholism [drinking his pay], Gram hired herself out to a farm family where one of her more onerous duties was making lye soap. Her son, Bernard, was with her during that job, while Bernadine was hired out to work for the Bushey family. Bernadine was to take care of all the youngsters, including the babies still in diapers. In those days, the cloth diapers were soaked in cold water and had to be rung out and washed by hand. Bernadine soon developed a skin infection on her hands from the process. Unable to cope with the problem and afraid to say anything to the Bushey's she, at the age of 16, ran away from their house without anyone's knowledge. She knew she couldn't walk the twenty miles to where her mother was living, but she did make it the eight miles to her uncle's house. It was raining during her trip and besides getting soaked, she hid in the ditches when cars came by so they wouldn't see her. When she arrived, no one was home at her uncle's house, so she sat on the front porch steps to wait. Someone driving by saw her there and told her uncle, letting him know there was a young girl sitting on his front steps. Soon, he collected her and brought her back home, where she gathered her things and went to live with Verdi Marstol for the last two years of high school during the early 1940s [the beginning of the World War II years].

BERNADINE MARIE worked for Capper Publications, Inc, after she graduated in 1943 from the Immaculate Conception High School at St. Marys, Pottawatomie County, Kansas. She worked there as a secretary from June 1943 through 1944. Capper

Publications was owned by then U. S. Senator Arthur Capper (Republican) of Kansas. At that time the publishing company published most of the major newspapers and farming magazines in Kansas.

BERNADINE MARIE sold her home at Antietam Drive, Fairfax, Fairfax County, Virginia after the death of her husband. She moved into an apartment at Annandale, Fairfax County, Virginia. In 1978 she moved to another apartment at Countryside, Sterling, Loudoun County, Virginia. In April 1990 she purchased an apartment condominium at Port St. Lucie, St. Lucie County, Florida and moved there in June 1990, where she still resides [2015].

The Children of
Bernadine Marie Ozmer
and Robert Charles[4] Higgins

1. Donna Marie[5] Higgins

Bernadine Marie
with Donna Marie
(3 months)

born at 6:25 pm on June 29, 1946 at the Georgetown University Hospital at Washington, D.C. She was baptized on July 25, 1946 at St. Patrick's Catholic Church at Washington, D.C. by the Reverend Thomas A. Kelly C.S.C. Her sponsors at the baptismal were Roy W. Allen and Margaret Ozmer [her maternal aunt and uncle] and, by proxy, Anna Ozmer [nee Devader], her maternal grandmother.

Donna[5] married, first, Philip Alan[5] Coleman on August 10, 1968 at St. Leo's Catholic Church at Fairfax, Fairfax County, Virginia. The Reverend Walter F. Malloy performed the ceremony. Donna[5] and Philip[5] were divorced on August 19, 1976 at Fairfax, Fairfax County, Virginia. Philip[5] was born on September 26, 1945 at Washington, D.C. He died of respiratory arrest due to overwhelming infection caused by AIDS [Aquired Immune Deficiency Syndrome] at 7:00 pm on November 7,

1987 at the San Francisco General Hospital, San Francisco, California. His father was Leo Francis[4] [Oscar Joseph[3], Ernest Albert[2], William[1] {of Lewes, Susex, England}, (William[1]'s father is unknown; his mother was either Mary[1a] or Sarah[1a] Coleman), George[2a], Friend[3a]] Coleman of Topeka, Shawnee County, Kansas, and later of Landover, Prince Georges County, Maryland. His mother was Julia Elizabeth[2] [Charles[1] {of Miskol, Magyar/Hungary and later of the Borough of Manhattan, New York City, New York}] Kente of New York, New York, and later of Landover, Prince Georges County, Maryland. Donna[5] and Philip[5] had two children: Christopher Philip[6] and Kimberly Marie[6].

Donna[5] married, second, Stanton Darnbrook[10] Colson on April 2, 1977 at the Sheraton Inn at Reston, Fairfax County, Virginia. The Reverend James Miles of the Lake Ann Episcopal Congregation performed the ceremony. Stanton[10] was born on August 19, 1942 at Cahill House of the Cambridge City Hospital at Cambridge, Middlesex County, Massachusetts. His father was Douglas Herman[9] [Henry Wilson[8], Stanton E(phraim)[7], Theophilus T.[6] 2nd, Ephraim[5], Ichabod Downs[4], Hatevil[3], Samuel[2], Cornelius[1], Jan Cornelissen[1a] Van Rotterdam {of Rotterdam, Zud-Holland, The Netherlands}, Cornelius[2a] Jonckers] Colson of Brooklyn, New York and later of Boston, Suffolk

10

County, Massachusetts. His mother was Mary Elsie[2] {afa Elsie May} [William Irving[1] {of Cowansville, Province of Quebec, Canada}, Morris[1a], Franklin[2a] {of France}] Quebec of Manhattan, New York, New York, and later of Boston, Suffolk County, Massachusetts. Donna[5] and Stanton[10] currently [2015] reside at Weeksville, Pasquotank County, North Carolina. Stanton[10] adopted Christopher Philip[6] and Kimberly Marie[6] Coleman.

2. Sharon Ann[5] Higgins [a twin]
   born on December 17, 1950 at Washington, D.C. She married, first, Gerald Emmett O'Neill on September 18, 1971 in St. Leo's Catholic Church at Fairfax, Fairfax County, Virginia. They were divorced prior to 1977. Gerald was born on January 14, 1951 at San Diego, San Diego County, California. The name of Gerald's father is not known. His mother was (Unknown) Harnage. Sharon[5] and Gerald had no issue.

   Sharon[5] married, second, Thomas Wilhelm on May 13, 1978 at Tucson, Pima County, Arizona. Thomas was born on March 26, 1954 at Fort Wayne, Allen County, Indiana. His father was Robert C. Wilhelm of Fort Wayne, Allen County, Indiana and later of Tucson, Pima County, Arizona. His mother was Bettie Armor Wall of Rock Creek Township, Miner County, Indiana and later of Tucson, Pima County,

Arizona. Sharon[5] and Thomas currently reside [2015] at Las Flores, Orange County, California. Sharon[5] and Thomas had one daughter: Nichole Ann.

3. Karen Ellen[5] Higgins [a twin]
   born on December 17, 1950 at Washington, D.C. She married John Hugh Cheatham of Augusta, Richmond County, Georgia on June 19, 1971 in St. Leo's Catholic Church at Fairfax, Fairfax County, Virginia. John was born on January 26, 1948 at Savannah, Chatham County, Georgia. His natural father was John Hugh Brittain [who had a brother Harold Brittain]. John was adopted at age twelve. His adoptive father was Walter Cheatham of Savannah, Chatham County later of and North Augusta, Richmond County, Georgia. His adoptive mother was Martha Hazel [George Henry, Henry Clay, Ephraim {born circa 1803 in Georgia}] Cordle [who was orphaned at an early age after her parents died in a house fire] of Macon, Bibb County, Georgia. Karen[5] and John currently reside [2015] in a houseboat at Brannan Island, Isleton, Sacramento County, California. Karen[5] and John had two children: Clay Alan and Heather Marie.

Windsor Wilkerson "Jack" Ozmer

The Life and Times of
Windsor Wilkerson "Jack" Ozmer

PATERNAL ANCESTRY: [OZMER/OSMORE: Jefferson Gadwell, Robert Clark, Richard, (William)]

MATERNAL ANCESTRY: [HUNTER: Ella Jane]

WINDSOR WILKERSON was born on September 26, 1882 at Fairburn, Fulton County, Georgia. He died of acute coronary occlusion [Heart Attack] at 3:00 am on June 16, 1963 at Ault's Nursing Home at St. Marys,

Anna Emma Devader & Windsor Wilkerson Ozmer

Pottawatomie County, Kansas and was buried there in the Mount Calvery Cemetery. His father was Jefferson Gadwell Ozmer of DeKalb County and later of Fairburn, Fulton County, Georgia. His mother was Ella Jane Hunter of Georgia.

WINDSOR WILKERSON, who went by the nickname of "Jack," married Anna Emma[2] Devader of Morris, Wyandotte County, Kansas

15

on February 8, 1921 at Kinney Heights, Kansas City, Kansas. The ceremony was performed in the Sacred Hearts Catholic Church by William DeBoeck, Rector. Anna[2] was born on December 21, 1898 at Morris, Wyandotte County, Kansas. She died on May 13, 1983 at the residence of her daughter Bernadine Marie Higgins [nee Ozmer] at Annandale, Fairfax County, Virginia and was returned for burial at Mount Calvary Cemetery at Topeka, Shawnee County, Kansas. Her father was Peter Edward[1] [Jacobus-Francies[1a]] Duivetter of Belgium and later of Atkinson, Henry County, Illinois. Her mother was Prudanse[1] [Joseph E.[1a]] Cousman of St. Lauriens, Belgium and later of Atkinson, Henry County, Illinois.

Anna[2] had married, first, Charles Henry[3] Trezise on November 30, 1917 at Topeka, Shawnee County, Kansas by Ralph H. Gow, Probate Judge. Charles was born on May 24, 1893 near Emmett, Pottawatomie County, Kansas. He died of influenza on October 18, 1918 at the Army Barracks at State College, Solano County, New Mexico and was returned home for burial at Emmett, Jackson County, Kansas. His father was Henry P.[2] [Henry P.[1] {of St. Just, Cornwall, England}, Henry[1a], Henry[2a]] Trezise of England, later of Michigan and finally of Pottawatomie County, Kansas. His mother was Margaret Ellen [John] Songs [his father's fourth wife] of Andrew County, Missouri

16

and later of Jackson County, Kansas. Anna[2] and Charles[3] had a child: Charles Henry[4].

WINDSOR WILKERSON appeared on the 1900 U.S. Census, living at home in the Evans District of DeKalb County, Georgia. As a young man he spent many years away from home, wandering here and there to parts unknown. He was known to get up from the dinner table to go out for a pack of cigarettes and not return for several days. Upon returning, he would act as if nothing abnormal happened. There is even a story that one morning he got up from the breakfast table to go to work and didn't come back home for a year.

WINDSOR WILKERSON, more commonly known as "Jack," came from Georgia to Kansas City, Missouri when he was in his early thirties [probably circa 1913/1914] and found work as a mechanic. He then moved to Emmett, Jackson County, Kansas where he trained, then worked with Anna[2]'s first husband, Charles[3] Trezise. After Anna[2]'s husband died in 1918, "Jack" pestered her to marry him. He once told her that if she didn't agree to marry him that he would hang himself in a tree that was on the path where she walked to work. As another point of persuasion, he told her that he had prayed over Charlie[3]'s grave that if she married him that he would take good care of her. "Jack" must have returned to visit his family in

Georgia, for in 1920 [as reported by a descendant] he and his father visited relatives in Texas.

WINDSOR WILKERSON and Anna[2] were finally married in 1921 and they removed to St. Marys, Pottawatomie County, Kansas where he was a resident until his death. He was regarded as one of the best auto mechanics in the area. He retired as a mechanic in 1953 and died ten years later at Ault's Nursing Home at St. Marys, Pottawatomie County, Kansas.

The Children of
Windsor Wilkerson Ozmer
and Anna Emma[2] Devader

1. Margaret Ella Leotha "Peg" Ozmer
   born on October 4, 1922 at St. Marys, Pottawatomie County, Kansas. She married Roy William[2] Allen on February 23, 1946 in the Assumption Catholic Church at Topeka, Shawnee County, Kansas. Roy[2] was born on May 1, 1921 at St. Marys, Pottawatomie County, Kansas. He died on October 2, 2002 at Topeka, Shawnee County, Kansas and was buried there in Mt. Calvary Cemetery. His father was Ernest Gotfried[1] [Turie E.[1a] {afa Trure E.}] Allen of Vadstena, Gotland, Sweden [Editor's Note: Vadstena is a small town noted for its lace. It is located on the island of

Gotland on the east coast of Sweden, south of Stockholm]. His mother was Mary Martha[2] [Henry[1] {of Germany}] Eichman [his second wife] of Flush, Pottawatomie County, Kansas. Margaret currently resides [2015] at Topeka, Shawnee County, Kansas. Margaret and Roy[2] had three children:

a. Linda Marie[3] Allen
born on February 17, 1949 at Topeka, Shawnee County, Kansas. She married William Gene "Bill" Clark on July 18, 1970 at Carson City, Ormsby County, Nevada. The marriage was recorded there on July 24, 1970. He was born on September 1, 1944 at Concord, Contra Costa County, California. His father was Laurel Clark [who died when "Bill" was age 15] of Contra Costa County, California. His mother was Ruth Stone of Contra Costa County, California. Linda and Bill had two children:

1. Angie Marie Clark
born on December 24, 1971 at Topeka, Shawnee County, Kansas.

2. Andrew William "Andy" Clark
born on March 18, 1975 at Topeka, Shawnee County, Kansas.

b. Patricia Ann[3] "Pat" Allen
born on July 6, 1952 at Topeka, Shawnee County, Kansas. She married Ronald Gene[5] "Ron" Luedke in 1973 at Colony, Anderson County, Kansas. He was born on February 25, 1947 at Iola, Allen County, Kansas. His father was Robert Justin[4] [Charles Jesse[3] {of Shelby County, Illinois}, Philip N.[2] {of New York}, Carl[1] {of Germany}] of Scott City, Scott County, Kansas. His mother was Ruth E. Finley of Kansas. Pat[3] and Ron[5] had three children:

1. Laura Maria[6] Allen
born June 25, 1982 in Kansas.

2. Christopher Gene[6] Allen
born April 19, 1976 in Kansas

3. Michele Ann[6] Allen
date of birth in Kansas is not known.

c. Robert William[3] "Bob" Allen
born on February 22, 1965 at Topeka, Shawnee County, Kansas. He married April Welcome on October 29, 1993 at Topeka, Shawnee County, Kansas. She was born on December 3, (1967-1969) at Dayton, Montgomery County, Ohio. The name of her father and mother is not known. Bob[3] and April had a child:

1. Ashley Nicole Allen
   born January 31, 1994 at Topeka, Shawnee
   County, Kansas.

2. Bernadine Marie Prudence "Pud" Ozmer
born on November 4, 1925 at St. Marys, Potta-
watomie County, Kansas. She married Robert
Charles[4] Higgins on July 23, 1945 at Washington,
D.C. Robert[4] was born on March 16, 1925 at
Washington, D.C. He died of lung cancer on
February 19, 1982 at home at Fairfax, Fairfax
County, Virginia. His father was Joseph Francis[3]
[John Joseph[2], John[1] {of Ireland}] Higgins of
Schenectady, Schenectady County, New York and
later of Washington, D.C. and Alexandria, Vir-
ginia. His mother was Margaret Ellen [William
Henry, Alvah, William, Joseph, Joseph {of Massa-
chusetts}] Pitts of Castleton, Rennselaer County,
New York. Bernadine and Robert[4] had three
children: Donna Marie[5], Sharon Ann[5] [a twin] and
Karen Ellen[5] [a twin].

3. LeRoy Robert Ozmer
   born on December 5, 1928 at St. Marys, Pottawatomie County, Kansas. He died of chicken pox
as an infant on November 17, 1929 at St. Marys,
Pottawatomie County, Kansas.

4. Bernard Francis James Ozmer
   born on November 30, 1931 at home on Palmer

Street at St. Marys, Pottawatomie County, Kansas. He died of lung cancer at 3:00 pm on December 17, 1986 at his home at Emmett, Gem County, Idaho. At his request, he was cremated and his ashes were spread on the grave of his son, Steven Christopher, in the Queen of Haven Catholic Cemetery at LaFayette, Contra Costa County, California. The ashes were spread by Bernard's second wife, Gerrie, who had to sneak into the cemetery at night to accomplish the task. He married, first, Jeannette Irene[3] Dureault on May 30, 1956 at Tucson, Pima County, Arizona. They were later divorced in October 1975 [another researcher says March 1976] at Martinez, Contra Costa County, California. Jeannette[3] was born on January 14, 1938 at Westford, Middlesex County, Massachusetts. Her father was Armand R.[2] [Aime[1] {afa Eurie Durot of Tingwick, Athabaska, Quebec Province, Canada and later of Lowell, Middlesex County, Massachusetts}, Emelie-Onezine[1a] {afa Onesime of Puisieulx, France}] Dureault of Lowell, Middlesex County, Massachusetts and later of Tucson, Pima County, Arizona. Her mother was Irene Alice[2] [Joseph Etienne[1] {of Nicolet, Quebec Province, Canada}, Adolphe[1a], Jean B.[2a], Louis F.[3a], Augustin[4a] {of Quebec, Quebec Province, Canada}, Louis[5a] {Parmentier Lyonnais {of Lyon, Rhone, Rhone-Alpes, France}] Parmentier of Lowell, Middlesex County, Massachusetts and later of

Tucson, Pima County, Arizona. Bernard and Jeanetta[3] had five children:

a. Bernard Francis "Buddy" "Bud" Ozmer, Jr.
born on April 6, 1957 at Topeka, Shawnee County, Kansas. He married Genneace Slagle [afa Janice Cosh] on June 20, 1975. They were divorced on October 10, 1981 in Contra Costa County, California. Bernard and Genneace had one child:

1. Jason Bernard "Jase" Ozmer
born on July 24, 1976 in Alabama. He married Yajahida Alicia Acuna on May 14, 2004 at Mesa, Maricopa County, Arizona.

Bernard married, second, Denise Audene[12] Bigelow on June 17, 1987 at Reno, Washoe County, Nevada. She was born on September 29, 1961 at San Leandro, Alameda County, California. She died on September 11, 1995 at Boise, Ada County, Idaho. The funeral card, dated September 13, 1975 at the Summers Funeral Home at Boise read as follows:

After Glow

"I'd like the memory of me to be a happy one,
Id' like to leave an afterglow of smiles when life
is done,

I'd like to leave an echo whispering softly down
the ways,
Of happy times and laughing times and bright
and sunny days,
I'd like the tears of those who grieve to dry
before the sun,
Of happy memories that I leave when life is
done.

Her father was Harmon Spencer[11] [Herbert
S.[10], Harmon Elmer[9] {of Somerset County,
Maine}, Calvin[8], James[7], James S.[6] {of
Templeton, Worcester County, Massa-
chusetts}, James[5] {of Weston, Middlesex
County, Massachusetts}, James[4], Jonathan[3],
Joshua[2], John[1] {of Wrentham, Suffolk,
England}, Randall[1a] {of Ollerton, Knutsford,
Cheshire, England}, Robert[2a] {de Baguley},
Randall[3a], Ralph[4a] {of Baguley, Bucklow,
Cheshire, England}, Hamon[5a] {born circa
1470 of Knutsford Booth, Bucklow, Cheshire,
England}] Bigelow of San Leandro, Alameda
County, California. Her mother was Audene
(Unknown). There was no issue.

Bernard married, third, Sarah Hoene on
April 28, 2001 at Boise, Ada County, Idaho.
They were divorced in February 2005 at
Boise, Ada County, Idaho. She was born on
July 25, 1973 at Grangeville, Idaho County,
Idaho. Her father was Dennis M. Hoene. Her

24

mother was Paula Silvestri. Bernard and Sarah had a child:

2. Samantha Danielle Ozmer
   born on August 1, 2004 at Nampa, Canyon County, Idaho.

Bernard, then of Caldwell, Canyon County, Idaho, married, fourth, Kathleen Mary "Kathy" Morgan on September 10, 2011 at Cartagena, Colombia. Bernard and Kathleen were living at Cascade, Valley County, Idaho [2014]. Bernard and Kathleen had no issue.

b. Michael Lee Ozmer
   born on October 5, 1959 at Tucson, Pima County, Arizona. He married Pamela Joanne[4] Berthold on June 29, 1981 [another researcher says August 22] at Carson City, Carson County, Nevada [they were residents of Martinez, Contra Costa County, California]. They divorced circa 1987 at Oregon City, Clackamas County, Oregon. Her father was (Unknown)[3] [Otto Fredrick[2] {of Medford, Taylor County, Wisconsin and later of Oregon City, Clackamas County, Oregon}, William Robert[1] {of Gruen-Lichtenberg, Saxony, Germany and later of Carnby,

Clackamas County, Oregon}, Fredrich W.[1a], Fredrich W.[2a]] Berthold of Clackamas County, Oregon. The name of her mother is not known. Michael and Pamela[4] were living at Cascade, Valley County, Idaho [2014]. Michael was a deputy sheriff and a U. S. postal carrier. Michael and Pamela[4] had three children:

1. Joseph Steven Ozmer
   born on August 28, 1982 at Martinez, Contra Costa County, California. Joseph married (Unknown). Joseph and (Unknown) had a child:

   a. Taylor Marie Ozmer
      born circa March 1998 in California.

   Joseph married, second, Lindsey Anne Garber on February 18, 2001 in Deschutis County, Oregon. Joseph and Lindsey had a child:

   b. Joey Ozmer
      born on October 15, 2000.

2. Faith Elizabeth Ozmer
   born on September 30, 1983 at Chester, Plumas County, California. She married

Jesus Garcia Guerrero II in Bend County, Colorado. They were divorced in October 2004 in Oregon. He was born on June 28, 1975 at Michloacan Province, Mexico. The name of his father and mother is not known. Faith and Jesus had two children:

a. Mariah Faith Guerrero
    born on November 13, 1999 in the St. Charles Medical Center at Bend, Deschutes County, Oregon.

b. Jesus Garcia Guerrero III
    born on May 8, 2001 in the St. Charles Medical Center at Bend, Deschutes County, Oregon.

Faith married, second, Sean Michael Bast on September 22, 2006 in Marion County, Oregon.

Faith married, third, Christopher Brewer. They lived in Oregon [2014]. Faith and Christopher have a child: Dellilah.

3. Michael Lee "J.R." Ozmer, Jr.
    born on July 25, 1985 at Mt. Vernon, Lawrence County, Missouri. He married, in a civil ceremony, Judith A. "Judy"

Raine in the spring of 2001 at Boise, Ada County, Idaho. Earlier, on July 13, 1999, they had celebrated their common union at Cascade, Valley County, Idaho. She was born on March 29, 1960 at Los Angeles [city of], California. Her father's name is not known. Her mother was (Unknown) Shafer. Michael and Judy had no issue.

Judy had married, first, Craig N. Porter on February 24, 1979 in Kern County, California. Judy and Craig had four children: Don, Chris, James and Joseph.

Michael Lee married, second, Claudette Anne McDonald on October 23 [another researcher says October 30th], 2009 at Portland, Multnomah County, Oregon. Michael and Claudette had a child: Michael Lee [Editor's Note: When they married, Claudette had a child: Dyani].

Pamela[4] Berthold had married, first, (Unknown) Ruddock. Pamela and (Unknown) Ruddock had one child: Jason Mare.

Pamela[4] had married, second, Terry Craig Harris on December 2, 1989 in Clackamas

County, Oregon. He was born on May 1, 1963 in Oregon.

c. Steven Christopher Ozmer
born on August 19, 1961 at Tucson, Pima County, Arizona. He died, age 17, of lymphoma on September 13, 1978 at Concord, Contra Costa County, California and was buried there in the Queen of Heaven Catholic Cemetery at Lafayette. At his funeral, his mother offered the following poem by Kahlil Gibran:

> "He shall not grow old,
> As we who are left grow old,
> Age shall not weary him,
> Nor the years condemn,
> At the going down of the sun,
> And in the morning,
> We shall remember him."

d. David William Ozmer [a twin]
born on March 5, 1963 at Concord, Contra Costa County, California. He married Gina M. Carrasco of California on November 7, 1982 at Reno, Washoe County, Nevada. They divorced circa 1987 in Solano County, California. She was born on June 29, 1956 at San Diego [city of], California. David was a

security systems mechanic/installer. David and Gina had two daughters:

1. Dawnine Elana Ozmer
   born on December 4, 1983 at Walnut Creek, Contra Costa County, California. She married Dustin Foster on July 31, 2004 at Idaho City, Boise County, Idaho. Dawnine and Dustin had a child: Robert Dean.

2. Andrea Delphine Ozmer
   born on September 25, 1985 at Walnut Creek, Contra Costa County, California. She married Tim Landon on January 7, 2008 at Boise, Ada County, Idaho. He was born on April 19, 1980. Andrea and Tim had a child: Damien Eugene.

e. Debra Ann "Debbie" Ozmer [a twin]
   born on March 5, 1963 at Concord, Contra Costa County, California. She married Mark Douglas Pacini of California on October 16, 1983 at Stateline, Douglas County, Nevada. They divorced. He was born on April 2, 1961 in Contra Costa County, California. Debra was living at Pittsburg, Contra Costa County, California [2012]. Debra and Mark had two children:

1. Steven Pacini
    born on June 18, 1986 at Martinez, Contra Costa County, California.

2. Brittnee Anne Pacini
    born on March 23, 1996 at Concord, Contra Costa County, California.

Jeannette[2] "Jean" married, second, Scott Carson[11] Wells on September 30, 1982 at Watford, Herfordshire, England. Scott[11]was born on February 11, 1940 at Los Angeles, Los Angeles County, California. His father was Scott Carson[10] [Ebenezer[9] {afa Ebenezer of South Carolina}, Eliza Sewell[8] Wells {who had Ebenezer by Henry Lawrence Britton of South Carolina, who died in the U. S. Civil War during the Battle of Manassas}, Ebenezer[7] of Warren, Knox County, Maine}, Ebenezer[6], Robert[5], Nathaniel[4] {of Newbury, Essex County, Massachusetts}, Thomas[3], John[2] {of Ipswich, Essex County, Massachusetts, Thomas[1] {of Essex County, England}, Thomas[1a] {of Essex, Lancaster, England}, Thomas[2a]] Wells, Sr. of California. His mother was Lila Mary [Ponciano J. "Ponce" of Idaho}] Jimenez of Sacramento, Sacramento County, California. Jean[2] and Scott[11] had no issue.

Bernard married, second, Geraldine Rae[6] "Gerrie" Clure on March 16, 1979 and the marriage was recorded on March 19, 1979 at Reno, Washoe County, Nevada. Geraldine[6] was born on November 21, 1950 in St. Patrick's Hospital at Missoula, Missoula County, Montana [Editor's Note: The family actually lived at Stephen's Mountain]. Her father was Kenneth Miller[5] [Asher Enos[4] {of Crawford, Dawes County, Nebraska}, John Baptiste[3] {of Naperville, Dupage Counthy, Illinois}, Joseph[2] {of Canada and later of Iowa}, John[1] {born circa 1790/1795 of Switzerland and later of Canada and finally of Minnesota, where he died in 1862}] Clure of Laramie County, Wyoming. Her mother was Ruby Patricia[3] [Jonas A.[2] {afa Joseph of Verona, Lawrence County, Missouri}, William[1] {of England and later of Missouri}] Garrod of Hamilton, Ravelli County, Montana. Bernard and Geraldine[6] had no issue.

Geraldine[6] married, first, Russell Clifford Terry. They later divorced. His father was Hillard H. Terry of Colorado. His mother was Maxine (Unknown) of Colorado. Geraldine[6] and Russell had a child: Ginger Rae Terry.

Geraldine[6] married, second, Wallace Edgar Martin of Oklahoma on March 15, 1972 in

Humboldt County, Nevada. The marriage was recorded there on March 23, 1972. They later divorced. His adoptive father was William Martin of Alabama. His mother was Dolly (Unknown). There was no issue.

Geraldine[6] married, fourth, Danny Leo Green on November 28, 1987 [recorded on December 2, 1987] in Clark County, Nevada. They later divorced. His father was Thomas Leo Green of Ada County, Idaho. His mother was Harriet May Lake of Ada County, Idaho. There was no issue.

Geraldine[6] married, fifth, Bernard Vincent Montgomery on October 4, 1994 in Yamhill County, Oregon. They later divorced. There was no issue.

Jefferson Gadwell Ozmer

The Life and Times of Jefferson Gadwell Ozmer

PATERNAL ANCESTRY: [OZMER/OSMORE: Robert Clark, Richard, (William)]

MATERNAL ANCESTRY: [GRAHAM: Elizabeth[4], "Reverend" Robert Windsor[3] {of Richmond County, Virginia}, William Grimes[2], George[1] {of Scotland}, John[1a] {a schoolmaster of County Down, Ireland}]

JEFFERSON GADWELL was born on September 26, 1851 in DeKalb County, Georgia. He died on November 8, 1939 at Fairburn, Fulton County, Georgia and was buried, along with his two wives, one on each side of him, in the Wesley Chapel Methodist Church Cemetery in DeKalb County, Georgia. His father was Robert Clark Osmore of DeKalb County, Georgia. His mother was Elizabeth[4] Graham of North Carolina and later of DeKalb County, Georgia.

[EDITOR'S NOTE: With this generation the surname, also found in the records as OSMORE, OSMOORE, and OZMORE, became OZMER, and the rest of his brothers and sisters are generally known by OZMER or OZMORE]

JEFFERSON GADWELL married, first, Ella Jane Hunter on November 9 (11), 1877 in DeKalb County,

Georgia by W.R. Foot [Editor's Note: Foot signed the marriage license but did not indicate his title]. Ella was born on February 13, 1858 in Georgia. She died on November 3, 1901 in DeKalb County, Georgia and was buried there in the Wesley Chapel Methodist Churchyard. Her father was LeRoy G. [Ferisa {of Georgia}] Hunter of Evans, DeKalb County, Georgia. Her mother was Susan M. [Josiah D. {of South Carolina}] Longford of North Carolina.

JEFFERSON GADWELL married, second, his niece, Pamelia Elizabeth [afa Permelia] Ozmer. The date and place of their marriage is not known. Pamelia was born on May 16, 1859 in DeKalb County, Georgia. She died on July 6, 1931 [another record says she died on November 3, 1931], in DeKalb County, Georgia and was buried in the Wesley Chapel Methodist Church Cemetery in DeKalb County, Georgia. Her father was John Windsor [Robert Clark, Richard {of Brunswick County, Virginia}, (William)] Osmore of Henry County [later DeKalb County], Georgia [Editor's Note: this was Jefferson Gadwell's brother]. Her mother was Elizabeth Parr[5] [William[4] {of North Carolina and later of Georgia}, John[3], Thomas[2] {of Sussex County, Virginia}, William[1] {of London, England}] Mitchell of DeKalb County, Georgia.

JEFFERSON GADWELL is found on the 1860 U. S. Census living at Evans Street of the Panthersville

38

District, DeKalb County, Georgia with his mother and his other siblings.

JEFFERSON GADWELL is found on the 1870 U.S. Census in the Barns District, Flat Rock, DeKalb County, Georgia as a farm laborer, living with the family of John W. Ozmore [his brother].

JEFFERSON GADWELL appears on the 1900 U.S. Census, age 48, living in the Evans District of DeKalb County, Georgia along with his wife, Ella J, age 42, and his children, Windsor W, age 17, Sallie Sue, age 12, Annie G, age 6, and Roy R., age 1.

Jefferson Gadwell Ozmer his sister, Susan Jane

JEFFERSON GADWELL was regarded as a frugal man. He once told his son, Roy, "Son! If there's ever anything you need, no matter how hard it is to find or how much it costs, you just get word to me, and I'll tell you how to get along without it."

The Children of
Jefferson Gadwell Ozmer
and Ella Jane Hunter

1. Hattie Lee Ozmer
   born on August 31, 1878 at Fairburn, Fulton County, Georgia. She died as a child on March 6, 1886 at Fairburn, Fulton County, Georgia and was buried there in the Wesley Chapel Methodist Church Cemetery.

2. **Windsor Wilkerson "Jack" Ozmer**
   born on September 26, 1882 at Fairburn, Fulton County, Georgia. He died on June 16, 1963 at St. Marys, Pottawatomie County, Kansas. He married Anna Emma[2] Devader on February 8, 1921 at Kinney Heights, Kansas City, Kansas. Anna[2] was born on December 21, 1898 at Morris, Wyandotte County, Kansas. She died on May 13, 1983 at the residence of her daughter, Bernadine Marie Higgins [nee Ozmer], at Annandale, Fairfax County, Virginia. Anna[2]'s father was Peter Edward[1] [Jacobus-Francies[1a]] Duivetter of Watervliet, Belgium and later of Atkinson, Henry County, Illinois. Her mother was Prudanse[1] [Joseph E.[1a]] Cousman of St. Lauriens, Belgium and later of Atkinson, Henry County, Illinois. Windsor and Anna[2] had four children: Margaret Ella Leotha "Peg," Bernadine Marie Prudence "Pud," LeRoy

Robert and Bernard Francis James.

Anna[2] had married, first, Charles Henry[3] "Charley" Trezise on November 30, 1917 at Emmett, Pottawatomie County, Kansas. Charles[2] was born on May 24, 1893 near Emmett, Pottawatomie County, Kansas. He died, age 25 years, 4 months, 22 days, of influenza on October 18, 1918 at the Army Barracks at State College, Mecilla Park, Solano County, New Mexico and was returned home for burial at Emmett, Pottawatomie County, Kansas. His father was Henry P.[2] [Henry P.[1] {of St. Just, Cornwall, England}, Henry[1a], Henry[2a]] Trezise of England and later of Michigan and finally of Pottawatomie County, Kansas. His mother was Margaret Ellen [John] Songs [his father's fourth wife] of Andrew County, Missouri and later of Jackson County, Kansas. Anna[2] and Charles[3] had one child: Charles Henry[4] [who was born on August 27, 1918 and who died, an infant, on October 10, 1918].

3. Sally Sue Ozmer
   born on February 15, 1888 at Fairburn, Fulton County, Georgia. She died in August 1985 at Plains, Sumter County, Georgia. She married William Joseph "Bill" Cannaday on November 19, 1912 at Fairburn, Fulton County, Georgia. William was born on August 4, 1886 at Fairburn, Fulton

County, Georgia. He died on March 22, 1921 at Fairburn, Fulton County, Georgia. His father was James Monroe Taylor [John {of Patrick County, Virginia}, William {Canada}, James, William] Cannaday of Fulton County, Georgia. His mother was Barbara Ann Driggers of Georgia. Sally and William lived at Plains, Sumter County, Georgia. Sally and William had three children:

a. Sarah Angella Cannaday
   born on August 23, 1913 at Fairburn, Fulton County, Georgia. She died on October 8, 1998 at Americus, Sumpter County, Georgia. She married M. H. Sewell on December 1, 1935 at Fairburn, Fulton County, Georgia. He was born on July 31, 1910 at Newell, Charlton County, Georgia. He died on November 17, 1975 at Americus, Sumpter County, Georgia. His father was Raymond [Harvey] Sewell of Georgia. His mother was Leona Lewellyn Monroe, James H. {of South Carolina}] Smith of Cowetta County, Georgia. Sarah and M. H. had three children: Barbara Anne, James Lee and Sara Janelle.

b. Clara Burrell [afa Curelle] Cannaday
   born circa 1917 in Campbell County, Georgia. Her date and place of death is not known.

c. William Joseph "Billy" Cannaday, Jr.
born on March 23, 1921 in Georgia. He died on December 5, 1988 at Ojai, Ventura County, California. William married Dorothy Hoffman. William and Dorothy had three children: Robert Samuel, Lee William and Harvey Joseph.

4. Amis Grace "Annie" Ozmer
born on October 23, 1893 at Fairburn, Fulton County, Georgia. She died in August 1981 at Cleveland, White County, Georgia. She married Claude Cole[11] Boynton on August 20, 1911 in Georgia. Claude[11] was born on June 16, 1893 in Georgia. He died on November 13, 1954 in Union County, Georgia. His father was Hillard A.[10] [Elija Winston[9], Yancey[8], Elija Snow[7], Amos[6], Ephraim[5], "Deacon" Joseph[4], Joseph[3], John[2], William[1] {of England}] Boynton of Georgia [born 1872]. His mother was Sidney M. (Unknown) [born 1879]. Amis and Claude[11] lived at Blairsville, Union County, Georgia. Amis and Claude[11] had a child: Mary[12] [who married Clyde Wehunt and had a child named Claude].

5. Robert LeRoy "Roy" Ozmer
born on January 21, 1899 at Decater, DeKalb County, Georgia. He died by suicide after gassing himself [because he was old and going blind] on October 21, 1969 at Flagg Pond, Erwin, Unicoi

County, Tennessee. He willed his body to an Institution in Texas. He married Mamie Emmeline Willis on April 27, 1927 in Unicoi County, Tennessee. They were later divorced. Mamie was born on August 24, 1901 in Tennessee. She died on November 17, 1980 at Erwin, Unicoi County, Tennessee. Her father was William Jasper[6] [John Anderson[5] {of North Carolina}, Benjamin[4], Jr., Benjamin[3] {of Rutherford County, North Carolina}, Henry[2] {of Goochland County, Virginia}, William Robert[1] {of Oxfordshire, England}, John[1a] {of Benson, St. Helen, Oxfordshire, England}, Stantiall[2a] {born circa 1616}] Willis of Washington County [later Unicoi County], Tennessee. Her mother was Martha E. [Arthur] Guinn of Washington County [later Unicoi County], Tennessee.

In his early years, he joined the Merchant Marines where, it is said, he lied about his age to join. When "Roy" was in his mid twenties he was a forest ranger and was involved in a hiking club, In 1950 he located on Pelican Key, one of the outlying southwestern islands of the Everglades. Then, in 1960, after Hurricane Donna swept the key bare, he moved to Panther Key, where he was known as the "Hermit of Panther Key," located about ten miles from Everglades City and eighty five miles west of Miami, Dade County, Florida. There, a friendly dog, a prowling panther and thousands of

wild birds shared res-
idence and "Roy" wel-
welcomed visitors with
steaming cups of what he
called "kauphy." On a
driftwood slab hung be-
neath a seagrape tree,
"Roy" carved a quotation
from naturalist/philoso-
pher John Burroughs: "I
come here to find myself:
it's so easy to get lost in
the world." Interestingly

Roy Ozmer "The Hermit
of Panther Key"

enough, "Roy" wasn't the first person known as
the Hermit of Panther Key. Incredibly, John
Gomez, born circa 1781, who lived until 1900, and
who served under Zachary Taylor at the Battle of
Lake Okeechobee, was known by that sobriquet.
Before isolating himself in the everglades, "Roy"
had been a seaman, carpenter, newspaperman,
forest ranger and actor. He had told a student/
author that he "was a hermit not because he didn't
like people, but because of a personal problem."
The problem was alcoholism. He had separated
himself from his family and lived on the island in
hopes of curing himself. "I've forgone society," he
was quoted as saying, "but if the world wants to
come out and share a cup of coffee or talk over a
problem, it's all right with me." He left behind

poems and drawings as well.

Robert and Mamie[7] had one son:

a. Robert Sequoyah Ozmer
born on June 14, 1932 at Flag Pond, Unicoi
County, Tennessee. He married, first, Amalea[8]
Slagle of Erwin, Unicoi County, Tennessee on
December 22, 1952 at Unicoi County, Tenn-
essee. They were divorced on June 9, 1971 at
Reno, Washoe County, Nevada. She was born
circa 1934 [she was age 18 when married],
presumably in Unicoi County, Tennessee. Her
father was Kelsie[7] [David Garfield[6], Jesse Jeryl[5]
{of Washington County, Tennessee}, Jessie[4],
John[3] {of Frederick County, Maryland}, Henry[2],
Henry[1] {of Germany}, Johannes Christian[1a]]
Slagle of Madison, Rockingham County, North
Carolina and later of Unicoi County, Tennessee.
Her mother was Vertie Mildred[9] [Walter
Hezekiah[8], James W.[7] "Jim," Hezekiah[6] {of
Buncombe County, North Carolina}, Arthur[5] {of
Surry County, North Carolina}, John Peter[4] {of
Albemarle, Patrick County, Virginia}, Mathew[3],
John Adam[2], John Adam[1] {of Cambridgeshire,
Hunt, England}] Corn of Unicoi County,
Tennessee. Robert and Amalea[8] had two
children:

1. Gary Lynn Ozmer
born on October 28, 1953 in Unicoi County Tennessee. He married Diane Elaine Weakley on October 28, 1976 at Frederick, Frederick County, Maryland. She was born on July 27, 1955, presumably at Poolesville, Montgomery County , Maryland. Her father was Charles Weakley of Poolesville, Montgomery County, Maryland. Her mother was Norma (Unknown) of Poolesville, Montgomery County, Maryland. Gary and Diane had two children:

a. David Bryan Ozmer
born on July 24, 1978 in Maryland. He married Carol Haner. David and Carol had two children: Chance Ethan and Dylan Walker.

b. Amanda Marie Ozmer
born May 18, 1981 in Maryland. She married, first, to (name unknown). They had two children: Jeremy and Anna Marie.

Amanda married, second, Johnny Ray Lewis on January 9, 2009. Johnny had two children from a previous marriage: Kyle and Tommy.

2. Connie Deborah Ozmer
born on June 23, 1957 in Unicoi County, Tennessee. She married Larry Eugene Wise. His father was Grayson Wise. His mother was Mary (Unknown). Connie and Larry had a child: Christy Lynn [who married Rudy Lyles and had a child: Kaitlin].

Connie married, second, Juan Alberto Diaz on March 18, 1981 at Bennettsville, Marlboro County, South Carolina. They divorced. He was born on October 17, 1949 at Carolina, Puerto Rico. Deborah and Juan had three children:

a. Adam Alexis Diaz
born on August 21, 1983 at Fayetteville, Cumberland County, North Carolina. He married Sarah Michelle Russell on September 25, 2010. Adam and Sarah have a child: Micah [born May 5, 2011]. Sarah had a child from a previous relationship: Aubrey.

b. Eric Miguel Diaz
born on February 11, 1986 in Berlin, Germany. He married Charlotte Bekker on August 7, 2009. Eric and Charlotte had two children: Dylan Nathaniel and

(child).

c. Evan Alberto Diaz
born on March 13, 1987 in Berlin, Germany. He married Janette Walker on July 31, 2009. There was no issue [as of 2012].

Connie married, third, Jozef Petrus Maria "Jos" Beijer on October 2, 2010 at her maternal grandparent's house at Edward's Branch, Flag Pond, Unicoi County, Tennessee. The wedding took place under a huge, old black walnut tree where as a child she used to play. He was born on August 27, 1956 at 't Kalf, The Netherlands. His father was Jozef "Joop" Beijer of Zaandam, The Netherlands. His mother was Annie Willemse of Zaandam, The Netherlands. Deborah and Jos currently [2015] reside at Koog aan de Zaan, The Netherlands.

Robert married, second, Nellie Faye Harris on June 23, 1971 at Reno, Washoe County, Nevada. Nellie was born on June 22, 1937 in Erwin County, Tennessee. Her father was Charles Harris of Spivey Creek, Erwin, Unicoi County, Tennessee. Her mother was Pansy (Unknown) of Unicoi County, Tennessee.

Nellie had married, first, Kenneth Effler of Edwards Branch, Flag Pond, Unicoi County, Tennessee. Robert and Nellie had two children:

3. Timothy Lee Ozmer
   born on January 14, 1968 in Unicoi County, Tennessee [Editor's Note: Timothy was born while Nellie Fay was still married, but Robert Ozmer always claimed him as his son and had his name changed from Harris to Ozmer]. He married Connie Johnson. Timothy and Connie had two children: Emily and Elizabeth.

4. Robbin Rene Ozmer
   born on November 27, 1972 at Crete, Saline County, Nebraska. She married Delbert Mears. They divorced. Robbin and Delbert had a child: Shelby Lynn.

No. 37.]

MARRIAGE LICENSE.

STATE OF GEORGIA, DeKalb COUNTY.

To any JUDGE, JUSTICE OF THE PEACE, OR MINSTER OF THE GOSPEL:

You are Hereby Authorized to Join

J. G. Ozmer and Ella Hunter

In the Holy State of Matrimony, according to the Constitution and Laws of this State; and for so doing, this shall be your sufficient License.

And you are hereby required to return this License to me, with your Certificate hereon of the fact and date of the Marriage.

Given under my hand and seal, this 9th day of *November* 187 7

H. W. Bayne [L.S.]
Ordinary.

GEORGIA, DeKalb County.

I CERTIFY, That *J. G. Ozmer* and *Miss Ella Hunter* were joined in matrimony by me, this 11th day of *Nov* Eighteen Hundred and Seventy 7

W. R. Foot — Past J
Ordinary.

Recorded:

Marriage License for
Jefferson Gadwell Ozmer
and Ella Jane Hunter

51

The Life and Times of
Robert Clark Osmore

PATERNAL ANCESTRY: [OSMORE: Richard, (William)]

MATERNAL ANCESTRY: [WADE: Susan, (Edward?)]

[EDITOR'S NOTE: Robert Clark Osmore is sometimes found in records spelled as Ausmore, Osmore, Ozmer and Ozmore]

ROBERT CLARK was born circa 1810 in Brunswick County, Virginia. He died, age 48, on April 25, 1858, in DeKalb County, Georgia and was buried there in the Wesley Chapel Methodist Church Cemetery. His father was Richard Osmore of Brunswick County, Virginia. His mother was Susan Wade of Brunswick County, Virginia.

ROBERT CLARK married Elizabeth[4] Graham on October 21, 1831 in Henry County [later known as DeKalb County], Georgia. Elizabeth was born in 1812 in North Carolina. She died on August 5, 1869 at DeKalb County, Georgia and was buried there with her husband in the Wesley Chapel Methodist Church Cemetery. She was standing under a tree during a storm, holding her youngest son, Robert, when both

53

were struck by lightening and killed. Her father was "Reverend" Robert Windsor[3] [William Grimes[2], George[1]{of Scotland}, John[1a] {a schoolmaster of County Down, Ireland}] Graham, a traveling minister who was born about 1790 in Richmond County, Virginia, and who died on January 21, 1865 and is buried at McDonough, Henry County, Georgia. Her mother was Chrissie[3] "Kiddy" [Joshua[2] {of Brunswick County, Virginia and later of the Marlboro District of South Carolina}, John George[1] {of Switzerland, and later of Weurttenburg, Germany}, Jacob[1a] {known as Amon of Zurich, Switzerland}, Jorle[2a] {Ammann}] Ammons of the Marlborough District of South Carolina. Elizabeth[4] is found on the 1860 U.S. Census [taken on July 24, 1860], age 45, at Decatur, Panthersville District, DeKalb County, Georgia as a domestic. She was enumerated along with eight of her children.

ROBERT CLARK participated in the 1832 Cherokee Land Lottery of Georgia. He is listed as a farmer and head of the military district where he lived. The land, Lot 232, 26th District, 3rd Section of Dearings, Henry County [which part later became Walton County], Georgia, was drawn in a lottery and granted sometime before January 1838.

ROBERT CLARK appears on the list of voters [as R. Ozmore] on the 1833 Henry County election returns as voter #106 of 156 voters. In 1847 he served on the DeKalb County Grand Jury.

ROBERT CLARK appears on the 1850 U.S. Census [taken October 19, 1850] as a farmer, age 40, born in Virginia, in the Panthersville District of DeKalb County, Georgia. He is enumerated along with his wife, Elizabeth[4], age 34, born North Carolina, and his children [all born Georgia], Martha, age 18, John W., age 15, Mary E., age 12, Sarah C., age 9, George S., age 7, Susan, age 5, and Laura, age 1.

ROBERT CLARK, whose death preceeded that of his wife, was spared the tragedy of his wife's and son's death together in an electrical storm. The May 20, 1858 issue of the Wesley Christian Advocate reported that Robert Ozmer died at his residence in DeKalb County, Georgia on April 25, 1858 in his 48th year. The article, written by Windsor[3] Graham, his father-in-law, goes on to say, "He joined the Methodist Church in 1843, of which he continued a faithful member until his death. The most of that time he served the church as a faithful and useful Class-lender. He lived so as to gain the love and confidence of all that knew him. His walk and conversation was godly. He was a kind husband and affectionate father and a good neighbor. He has left a wife, nine children, and many relatives to mourn their loss . . . ."

The Children of
Robert Clark Osmore
and Elizabeth[4] Graham

1. Martha Ann Osmore

born on August 13, 1833 in Henry County [later known as DeKalb County], Georgia. She died on December 4, 1911 in Georgia. She married Angus[3] McLeod on December 27, 1855 at Lylerly, Chattooga County, Georgia. He was born on December 26, 1826 in Decatur, Chattooga County, Georgia. He died of a stroke in 1909 in Lyerly, Chattooga County, Georgia. His father was Malcolm[2] [Neal[1] {of Gesto House, Gesto, Isle of Skye, Inverness, Scotland, United Kingdom who died at sea traveling to America}, Iain[1a]] McLeod of South Carolina and later of DeKalb County, Georgia. His mother was Rebecca [Hardiman] Rooks of South Carolina and later of DeKalb County, Georgia. Martha Ann and Angus[3] had eight children:

a. Mary Rebecca[4] McLeod

born on November 9, 1856 in DeKalb County, Georgia. She died on January 17, 1941 in Chatooga County, Georgia. She married Alfred J. Lee in 1877 in DeKalb County, Georgia. He was born on March 23, 1853 at Lyerly, Chattooga County, Georgia. He died on

October 4, 1922 in Floyd County, Georgia. His father was James J. Lee of Georgia. His mother was Mary J. (Unknown) of Georgia. Mary[4] and Alfred had nine children: Annie Belle, Benjamin F., Mary R., Sally M., Laura, Nellie G., Ruby B., Alfred L. and Hugh Malcolm.

b. Sarah Elizabeth[4] McLeod
born on August 23, 1858 in Georgia. Her date and place of death is not known. She married Alfred Rambo[9] Foster in 1881 in Georgia. He was born on August 11, 1860 in Chatooga County, Georgia. He died on January 8, 1896 at Thomasville, Thomas County, Georgia. His father was Kinchen Rambo[8] [Robert Sinclair[7] {of Abbeyville County, South Carolina}, John C.[6] {of Spartanburg County, South Carolina}, Moses[5] {of Amelia County, Virginia}, Thomas[4] of Essex County, Virginia}, Thomas[3], Robert[2] {of Gloucester County, Virginia}, Robert James[1] {Forster of Durham, England}, Robert[1a] {of Mundan, Hertfordshire, England}, Robert[2a]] Foster of Gwinnett County, Georgia. His mother was Melissa Ann[7] [Micajah[6] {of Fluvania County, Virginia}, Richard George[5] {of Middlesex County, Virginia}, James[4], Valentine[3], James[2] {of Isle of Wight County, Virginia}, William[1] {of Aberfielde, Berkshire, England}, William[1a] {of Marnhull, Dorset, England},

Richard[2a], Richard[3a]] Mayo of Floyd County, Georgia. Sarah[4] and Alfred[9] had seven children: Clara[10], Mary Ethel[10], Alison McLeod[10], E. Roy[10], Alfred G.[10], Annie Ruth[10] and Harold[10].

c. John Bethune[4] McLeod
born on October 15, 1860 in Georgia. He died on August 8, 1950 at Morrow, Clayton County, Georgia. He married Odessa Elwyn[8] Conine in 1892 in Clayton County, Georgia. She was born circa in March 17, 1874 in Clayton County, Georgia. She died on February 10, 1962 in Clayton County, Georgia. Her father was William Presley[7] [William Y.[6] {of Jackson County, Georgia}, Robert[5], David[4] {of New Jersey}, Dirck Richard[3] {of Cosacken County, New York}, Philip Leendertse[2] {of Schenectady, Schenectady County, New York}, Leendert Phillipse[1] {of Ghent, East Flanders, Belgium}, Phillip Konyn[1a] {born circa 1600}] Conine of Fayette County, Georgia. Her mother was Lucinda C. [John Madison {of Mechlinburg County, North Carolina}, William, Matthew {of Center, Guilford County, North Carolina}] Ozburn of Fayette County, Georgia. John[4] and Odessa[8] had nine children; Mattie Lou[5], Angus Conine[5], Robert Julian[5] "Jink," John Malcomb[5], Annie Margaret[5], Mildred Odessa[5], Edwin[5], Sarah Aliene[5] "Deenie" and Alfred DuBose[5].

d. Martha Ann Eliza[4] "Annie" McLeod
born on May 28, 1867 in Georgia. She died on December 8, 1904 in Chattooga County, Georgia. She married John A. Gilmer in 1889 in Georgia. He was born in December 1868 in Georgia. He died on April 30, 1932 in Floyd County, Georgia. The name of his father and mother is not known. Martha[4] and John had five children: Mary, Elwyn, Lillian, Rasser and Frank.

e. Robert Ozmer[4] McLeod
born on March 19, 1869 in Georgia. He died on October 14, 1953 at Chatooga County, Georgia. He married Mary Elizabeth "Mollie" Powell in 1899 in Chatooga County, Georgia. She was born on January 8, 1867 at Summerville, Chatooga County, Georgia [another researcher says she was born in Texas]. She died, age 74, on November 27, 1941 at Lyerly, Chatooga County, Georgia. Her father was Evan Absolom Powell of Georgia. Her mother was Margaret (Unknown) of Anderson County, South Carolina. Issue, if any, is not known.

f. Laura Priscilla[4] McLeod
born on August 28, 1871 in Georgia. She died on December 1, 1919 at Clarkson, DeKalb County, Georgia. She married Orville Asbury

[afa Asberry] Smith on November 10, 1892 in Georgia. He was born on August 13, 1867 in Georgia. He died on December 28, 1927 in DeKalb County, Georgia. His father was James MaHaffey [James, John, Cornelius] Smith of Georgia. His mother was Jane Caroline [Jacob, Edward] Callahan of Georgia. Laura[4] and Orville had nine children: Ethel McLeod, James Angus, Earnest Haygood, Annie Mabel, Martha Susan, Robert Orville and three others whose names are not known.

g. William Malcolm[4] McLeod
   born on August 31, 1873 in Georgia. He died on January 31, 1925 in South Carolina. He married Minnie Myrtle Jarnagin in 1899 in Georgia. She was born on January 9, 1878 at Cleveland, Bradley County, Tennessee. She died on March 30, 1937, possibly in South Carolina. Her father was Hamilton Thompson Jarnagin of Grainger County, Tennessee. Her mother was Sarah Elizabeth Johnson of Washington College, Washington County, Tennessee. William[4] and Minnie had four children: Malcom J.[5], Annie Elizabeth[5], Edith Dorothy[5] and William Angus[5].

h. Daniel Windsor[4] McLeod
   born on July 8, 1875 in Georgia. He died on May 11, 1930 in Chatooga County, Georgia. He

married Cynthia Ellen Strain in 1899 in Chatooga County, Georgia. She was born on March 2, 1879 in Georgia. She died on December 15, 1928 in Chatooga County, Georgia and was buried there in Lyerly. Her father was W. Harvey Strain of South Carolina. Her mother was Sarah F. Beavers of Georgia. Daniel[4] and Cynthia had two children: Sarah S.[5] and Barnaby[5].

2. John Windsor Osmore

born on November 17, 1835 [another researcher says 1836] in Henry County [later known as DeKalb County], Georgia. He died on August 28, 1915 at the home of his son, Robert Clark Ozmer [where he lived after the death of his wife], at Redan, DeKalb County, Georgia and is buried there in the Redan Town Cemetery. He married Elizabeth Parr[5] Mitchell on January 3, 1856 in DeKalb County, Georgia. Elizabeth[5] was born on June 20, 1838 in Georgia. She died on June 1, 1909 at Redan, DeKalb County, Georgia and is buried there in the Rock Chapel Cemetery. Her father was William[4] [John[3], Thomas[2] {of Sussex County, Virginia}, William[1] {of London, England}] of North Carolina and later of Georgia. Her mother was Malissa A. [Paschal C.] Phillips of Dekalb County, Georgia. John appears on the 1860 U.S. Census as an overseer [his wife, Elizabeth as a domestic], with 200 acres of property at New Redan, DeKalb County, Georgia valued at $1,200.00 [The property was located about five miles east of Stone Mountain and about one and a half miles off the Georgia railroad that ran east from Atlanta to August [Editor's Note: The location of his farm was probably the reason it was spared during General Sherman's march to Savannah]. He enlisted as a Private on July 26, 1862 and fought for the Confederacy in the U.S. Civil War, first in the 7th Georgia Regiment, then as a Sergeant in Company D, 42nd Regiment, Georgia Infantry. He appears on a register of CSA General Hospital No. 11, Charlotte, North Carolina. He was admitted March 4, 1865 and returned to duty March 8, 1865. He again appeared on the 1870 U.S. Census for DeKalb County, Georgia as a farmer. John and Elizabeth[5] had ten children:

a. Cornelia Elizabeth Ozmer
born on June 7, 1858 in DeKalb County, Georgia. She died on December 29, 1927 [another researcher says December 9, 1931] at Ellenwood, DeKalb County, Georgia and was buried there in the Masters Cemetery. She married John Zachary Taylor McKee on December 18, 1880 in DeKalb County, Georgia. He was born on April 4, 1847 at Panthersville, DeKalb County, Georgia. He died on February

12, 1937 in DeKalb County, Georgia. His father was Martin Capel [Samuel] McKee of Georgia. His mother was Mary Ann "Polly" Wilson of Abbeville County, South Carolina. Cornelia and John had seven children: Arthur Lovic, Robert Ozmer, Victor Hugo, Martin Windsor "Marty," Henry Grady, Thomas Taylor "Tom" and Mamie Elizabeth.

b. Lenora Louisa "Noley" Ozmer
born on September 25, 1860 in DeKalb County, Georgia. She died on June 10, 1916 in DeKalb County, Georgia. She married Paschal Crawford Evans on October 27 [another researcher says July 18th], 1878 in DeKalb County, Georgia [in 1880, they lived at Lithonia]. He was born circa 1859 in DeKalb County, Georgia. He died in 1923 in DeKalb County, Georgia. His father was William A. [James] Evans of DeKalb County, Georgia. His mother was Malissa A. Phillips of Georgia. Lenora and Paschal had at least two children: Ada and Robert Crawford.

c. John Herschel Ozmer
born on April 6, 1862 in DeKalb County, Georgia. He died of a cerebral hemorrhage on August 9, 1940 at Panthersville, DeKalb County, Georgia and was buried there in the Westview Cemetery. He married Georgia Lee

Owens on December 22, 1888 [another researcher says 1887] in DeKalb County, Georgia. She was born on July 13, 1867 at Panthersville, DeKalb County, Georgia. She died on June 23, 1942 in DeKalb County, Georgia and was buried there in the Westview Cemetery. Her father was Joseph S. [Benjamin {of South Carolina}] Owens of DeKalb County, Georgia. Her mother was Sarah Frances [James] Grant of DeKalb County, Georgia. In 1880, John was living with his brother John Windsor Ozmer, working as a farm laborer. A newspaper account dated Monday Evening, June 1916 featured an article about an indictment against John H. Ozmer for a double murder being dismissed for wont of evidence. He, along with Bryce Meredith Sprayberry were suspected of murdering William Harvey and Ann Grant Sprayberry [no further details have been found]. John and Georgia had two children: Lillian and Joseph Windsor.

e. Robert Clark Ozmer
born on April 30, 1867 in DeKalb County, Georgia. He died on April 17, 1919 at Decatur, DeKalb County, Georgia and was buried there in the Decatur City Cemetery. He married Mataline [afa Madeline] Vaughn on June 20, 1900 in DeKalb County, Georgia. She was born

in 1873 in Georgia. She died in 1949 [another researcher says December 1946] in DeKalb County, Georgia. The name of her father and mother is not known. Robert and Mataline had a child: Robert Vaughn.

f. Mary Etta Ozmer
born on August 25, 1869 in DeKalb County, Georgia. She died on July 30, 1894 in DeKalb County, Georgia and was buried there in the Wesley Chapel Methodist Cemetery.

g. William Angus Ozmer
born on August 17, 1872 in DeKalb County, Georgia. He died on November 19, 1952 at Decatur, DeKalb County, Georgia. He married, first, Madge Antoinette Medlock on October 21, 1900 in DeKalb County, Georgia [Editor's Note: Apparently, they were divorced by 1922]. She was born on February 8, 1881 [another researcher says 1880] at Atlanta, Fulton County, Georgia. She died on March 12, 1966 at Los Angeles, Los Angeles County, California. Her father was William P. [John Williams {of Greeenville County, South Carolina}, Isham {of Virginia}, John T. {of Henry County, Virginia}, John {of Abbeville, South Carolina}] Medlock of Gwinnett County, Georgia. Her mother was Vilenah Antoinette [William Pickney, William,

Robert Chester {of Farnham, Richmond County, Virginia}] Mason of Decatur, DeKalb County and later of Atlanta, Fulton County, Georgia. William and Madge had three children: Robert "Bob," William Angus, Jr. and Joseph Medlock.

William Angus married, second, Lucy Johnson on November 22, 1922 in DeKalb County, Georgia. She was born in 1875 [another researcher says circa 1901] at Decatur, DeKalb County, Georgia. Her date and place of death is not known. Her father was Daniel Noble [Daniel {of Elbert County, Georgia}] Johnson of Decatur, DeKalb County, Georgia. Her mother was Nancy Aldora Wheeler of Georgia. Issue, if any, is not known.

h. Martha Clara "Mattie" Ozmer
born on July 22, 1874 in DeKalb County, Georgia. She died on October 2, 1961 in DeKalb County, Georgia and was buried there in the Rock Chapel Methodist Church Cemetery at Lithonia. She married "Reverend" Francis Asbury[7] Ragsdale on February 7, 1897 in DeKalb County, Georgia [marriage book G, Page 128]. He was born on February 20, 1845 in DeKalb County, Georgia. He died on November 7, 1933 in DeKalb County, Georgia. His father was John C.[6] [Elijah[5] {of Mecklenburg

County, Virginia}, Peter[4] {of Prince George County, Virginia}, Benjamin[3], Godfrey[2] {of Jamestown, Henrico County, Virginia}, Godfrey[1] {of East Bridgeford, Notthinghamshire, England}, John[1a], William[2a], Henry[3a], Robert[4a] {of Ragdale, Leicestershire, England}, Henry[5a] {born circa 1460}] Ragsdale of DeKalb County, Georgia. His mother was Nancy Ann Lucas of DeKalb County, Georgia. Martha and Francis[7] had seven children: Forrest Asbury[8] [another record says Forrest Augustus[8]], Francis Clifford[8], Irene Elizabeth[8], James Winfred[8] [another record says James Winfrey[8]], Eugenia Capitola[8] "Jean," Martha Julia[8] and Robert Inman[8].

Francis[7] had married, first, Mary Frances Bowden on September 23, 1884 in Henry County, Georgia. She was born on April 2, 1867 in Henry County, Georgia. She died on March 12, 1896, either in Henry or DeKalb County, Georgia. The name of her father and mother is not known. Francis[7] and Mary had six children: Alverda[8], John Calhoun[8] [another record says John Clarence[8], a twin], Asbury Parks[8] [a twin], Elsie Kay[8], Jessie Burden[8] and Atticus Hugh[8].

i. Alice Clifford [afa Crawford] Ozmer born on January [another researcher says June]

26, 1876 in DeKalb County, Georgia. She died on August 13, 1967 at Atlanta, Fulton County, Georgia. She married Terrell Constantine Wesley on June 12, 1900 in DeKalb County, Georgia. He was born on February 3, 1870 in Gwinnett County, Georgia. He died on February 16, 1944 in Fulton County, Georgia and was buried there in the Westview Cemetery. His father was Pulaski Judge [Marvin Hammond {of Morgan County, Georgia}, John {of near the mouth of the Tar River, North Carolina}] Wesley of Newton County, Georgia. His mother was Louisa Elizabeth[5] [Terrell Constantine[4] {of South Carolina}, James[3] {of Abbeville County, South Carolina}, David Hazlep[2], James R.[1] {of Ireland}, James[1a]] Hawthorne of Gwinnett County, Georgia. Alice and Terrell had five children: Allen, Harry, John Wendel, Louise Elizabeth and Terrell Constantine, Jr.

j. Bessie Ozmer
born on September 8, 1878 in DeKalb County, Georgia. She died in 1944 in Georgia. She married Charles Ansel "Charlie" Rankin on December 13, 1899 in DeKalb County, Georgia. He was born circa 1860 in DeKalb County, Georgia. His date and place of death is not known. His father was John G. Rankin of

68

Massachusetts and later of Stone Mountain, DeKalb County, Georgia. His mother was Elizabeth A. (Unknown) of North Carolina. Bessie and Charles had six children: Ernest Gray, Elizabeth, Doris Louise, Charlie Ansel, Edith Rebecca and Katherine Cornelia.

k. Katheryn "Katie" Ozmer
born on March 7, 1882 at Redan, DeKalb County, Georgia. She died on November 6, 1962, possibly in Muscogee County, Georgia. She married Charles Oscar Wike on June 14, 1923 in DeKalb County, Georgia. He was born on July 13, 1880 in Greene County, Ohio. He died in July 1972 at Columbus, Muscogee County, Georgia. His father was Howard Thorn [George Kinard {of Pennsylvania}] Wike of Greene County, Ohio. His mother was Amanda Jane [David B. {of Pennsylvania}, John] Schaefer [afa Sheffer] of Greene County, Ohio. Katie and Charles had four children: Oscar Barkley, Charles Ozmer, Mary F. and Evelyn Elizabeth.

Charles had married, first, Estella May Barkley. The date of their marriage, probably in Greene County, Ohio, is not known. She was born on January 17, 1881 in Ohio. She died on July 12, 1917 and was buried at Clarksville, Clinton County, Ohio. Her father was John F. Barkley of

New Vienna, Clinton County, Ohio. Her mother was Lottie Parker of Hillsboro, Highland County, Ohio. Charles and Estella had one child: name not known.

3. Mary Elizabeth Osmore
   born on July 20, 1838 [another researcher says 1839] in DeKalb County, Georgia. She died on July 28, 1867 [another researcher says August 4, 1867, possibly the burial date] in DeKalb County, Georgia and was buried there in the Wesley Chapel Methodist Church Cemetery. She never married. She appears on the 1860 U.S. Census as a domestic in DeKalb County, Georgia. She was a member of the Sabbath School at Wesley Chapel.

4. Sarah Caroline Osmore
   born on April 30, 1841 in DeKalb County, Georgia. She died sometime after 1879 [another researcher says 1886] in Fayette County, Georgia. She married Thomas S.[5] "Tom" McGarity circa 1864/1866, probably in DeKalb County, Georgia. Thomas[6] was born on July 17, 1840 at McDonough, Henry County, Georgia. He died on October 14, 1919 at McDonough, Henry County, Georgia. What follows is an undated account of his death:

   "Mr. Tom McGarity, an aged citizen and Confederate solder died quite unexpectedly Thursday morning. He had been in feeble health for several months but recently had shown signs of considerable improvement. He had been residing at the home of his daughter, Laura Stonewall, but was brought to the home of his son, R. W. McGarity. On account of the apparent improvement in his condition, it was thought advisable to carry him to the Soldier's Home. His son put him in an automobile and started to the Home. When nearing the barracks he quietly passed away. He was livelier than usual that morning and was very enthusiastic over the proposition that he was to spend his last days among his old comrades who wore the gray.

Thomas[5]'s father was Wilson[4] [Abner John[3] {of Culpeper County, Virginia} John[2], Patrick[1] {of Ireland} Parick[1a]] McGarity of Elbert County, Georgia. His mother was Angeline[3] [Jeremiah[2] {of Orange County, Virginia}, John P.[1] {of Tralee, County Kerry, Ireland}, Patrick Joseph[1a]] McMullan of Elbert County, Georgia. Sarah appears on the 1860 U.S. Census as a domestic in DeKalb County, Georgia, presumably prior to her marriage to Thomas[5]. Sarah and Thomas[5] had five children:

a. Robert Wilson[6] McGarity
    born in 1868 at McDonough, Henry County,

Georgia. He married Ida Norton in 1889, probably in Campbell County, Georgia. She was born on November 23 1872 at Fairburn, Campbell County, Georgia. She died on November 17, 1938 at Fairburn, Campbell County, Georgia. Her father was Silas [Berry {of Richmond County, North Carolina}, William {of Northampton County, North Carolina} James {of Prince George County, Virginia}, William] Norton of Fayette County, Georgia. Her mother was Frances "Fanny" [Britton {of North Carolina}, Willis, James Robert] West of Fayette County, Georgia. Robert[6] and Ida had six children: James C.[7], Clyde E.[7], Carrie Frances[7], Minnie Vera[7], J. Windsor[7] and Robert Wilson[7].

b. Laura H.[6] McGarity

born on July 25, 1870 at McDonough, Henry County, Georgia. She died on May 18, 1907 in Fayette County, Georgia. She married John Willis Smith on January 30, 1890 in Fayette County, Georgia. He was born on September 18, 1870 in Fayette County, Georgia. He died on November 25, 1965 in Chatham County, Georgia. His father was James Madison [Thomas B.] Smith of Fayette County, Georgia. His mother was Martha [Britton {of North Carolina}, Willis, James Robert] West of Fayette County, Georgia. Laura[6] and John had four children; Lillie, William Pierce, Carrie Bell and (infant).

c. William Thomas[6] McGarity
    born on March 21, 1873 at McDonough, Henry County, Georgia. He died on October 9, 1939 at Fairburn, Fulton County, Georgia and was buried there in the Antioch United Methodist Church Cemetery. He married Dora Hunt on March 1, 1900 in Fayette County, Georgia. She was born circa 1873 in Georgia. She died on July 29, 1917 at Fairburn, Fulton County, Georgia and was buried there in the Antioch United Methodist Church Cemetery. The name of her father and mother is not known. William[6] and Dora had three children: Mary[7] and two others whose names are not known.

d. Sophia Elizabeth[6] "Sophie" McGarity
    born in April 1876 at McDonough, Henry County, Georgia. She died on April 18, 1942 in Henry County, Georgia. She married J. Hilliard Wyatt on November 22, 1896 in Fayette County, Gerogia. He was born in December 1856 in Henry County, Georgia. He died on May 27, 1939 in Fulton County, Georgia. His father was Joshua [Samuel, John] Wyatt of Henry County, Georgia. His mother was Miranda Elizabeth[4] [Christian[3] {of North Carolina}, Peter[2], Thomas[1]

{of England}] Lewis of Henry County, Georgia. Sophia[6] and J. Hilliard had six children: Lura, Jewel, Jesse Lawrence, John M., {possibly} Shane J. and one other whose name is not known.

e. Ida[6] McGarity
born in October 1879 at McDonough, Henry County, Georgia. Her date and place of death is not known.

5. George Smith Osmore
born on December 16, 1843 at Clarkston, DeKalb County, Georgia. He died on May 19, 1886 in DeKalb County, Georgia and is buried there in the Wesley Chapel Methodist Church Cemetery. He married Ella Jane Gunby of Georgia on January 13, 1870, probably at Panthersville, DeKalb County, Georgia. Ella was born in December 1847 in Georgia. She died on November 3, 1901 in DeKalb County [another researcher says Atlanta, Fulton County], Georgia and is buried there in the Wesley Chapel Methodist Church Cemetery. The name of her father and mother is not known. In 1860, he, a house carpenter, was living in DeKalb County, Georgia. George served as a Private in Company D, 42nd Regiment, Georgia Volunteer Infantry known as the DeKalb Rangers, Army of Tennessee, C.S.A. March 4, 1862. After the war, he lived for a

time in Atlanta [possibly from 1875 to early 1880], presumably when he secured work in rebuilding the city. On the 1880 U.S. Census he was living at Wild Cat, Cherokee County, Georgia. George and Ella had six children:

a. Ellie Gustenia "Gussie" Ozmer
   born in February 1872 in Cherokee County, Georgia. She died, age 86, on April 11, 1958 in Fulton County, Georgia. She married Edward L. Merchant on November 23, 1892 in Fulton County, Georgia.

b. Robert Edgar Ozmer
   born on December 1, 1873 in Cherokee County, Georgia. His date and place of death is not known. He married Cora Hudson sometime before 1908 [when their first child was born] in Fulton County, Georgia. She was born on December 3, 1881 in Georgia. Her date and place of death is not known. Her father was Thomas J. [William Jackson {of Greenville, Spartanburg County, South Carolina}, Lemur James] Hudson of Forsythe County, Georgia. Her mother was Martha (Unknown) of Georgia. Robert and Cora had two children: Robert Hudson and Richard Edgar.

c. Charles B. "Charlie" Ozmer
born on January 2 [another researcher says February 1st], 1876 at Atlanta, Fulton County, Georgia. He died, age 87, on March 31, 1963 in Richmond County, Georgia. He married Marion H. Campbell on July 18, 1906 in Fulton County, Georgia or. She was born on July 28, 1880 in Georgia. She died, age 95, on January 23, 1976 in Fulton County, Georgia. In 1910, Charles and Marion were living at Chattanooga, Hamilton County, Tennessee with their eight year old son, Horace. Her father was (Unknown) Campbell of Georgia. Her mother was Annie (Unknown) of Georgia. Soon after their son's birth, Charles and Marion relocated to Tennessee, but later returned to Georgia, where the lived until their death. Charles and Marion had a child: Horace.

Marion had married, first, Milo F. Wit [afa Witt and Witte] in 1893 at Atlanta, Fulton County, Georgia. He was born circa 1877/1879 at Stone Mountain, DeKalb County, Georgia. His date and place of death is not known [Editor's Note: However, he is probably one in the same as Miles F. Witt born circa 1877 who died, age 28, on October 7, 1905 at Atlanta, Fulton County, Georgia and buried there in the Oakland Cemetery; if so, his wife Marion either divorced or left him and had a child with Charles Ozmer before he died]. His father was Charlie C. Witt of Stone Mountain, DeKalb County, Georgia. The name of his mother is not known. Milo and Marion had two children: Charles E. and Marlo F.

d. Thomas Gunby Ozmer
born on March 19, 1879 at Atlanta, Fulton County, Georgia. He died on January 5, 1940 at Miami, Dade County, Florida. He married Sarah Ethel[3] McGiffin, probably circa 1900/1905 at Fernandina Beach, Nassau County, Florida. She was born on July 4, 1882 at Fernandina Beach, Nassau County, Florida. She died on December 9, 1957 at Fernandina Beach, Nassau County, Florida. Her father was James Hunter[2] [John[1] {of County Down, Ireland}}, James[1a]] McGiffin of Clover Township, Jefferson County, Pennsylvania. Her mother was Nancy [John] Girvin of Pennsylvania. Thomas and his family eventually moved to Waycross, Ware County, Georgia, then finally to Fernandina Beach, Nassau County, Florida, where he became the postmaster. Thomas and Sarah had three children: Thomas Gunby, Jr., Nancy Elizabeth and James McGiffin.

e. Christina Carly [afa Carrie] Ozmer
   [Another researcher calls her Mary Augusta]
   born on February 1, 1880 at Atlanta, Fulton
   County [another record says Cherokee County],
   Georgia. Her date and place of death is not
   known.

f. William "Willie" Ozmer
   born in December 1881 in Cherokee County,
   Georgia. His date and place of death is not
   known.

6. Susan Jane "Sue" Osmore
   born on April 4, 1846 [another research says 1845]
   in DeKalb County, Georgia. She died on April 7
   (5?), 1934 in DeKalb County, Georgia and is buried
   there in the Wesley Chapel Methodist Church
   Cemetery. She married George Washington[5]
   Crockett on July 14, 1867 in DeKalb County,
   Georgia. He was born on October 7, 1839 in Heard
   County, Georgia. He died on October 20, 1917 at
   Wesley Chapel, Fulton County, Georgia. His father
   was Samuel C.[4] [Joseph[3] {of Wythe County,
   Virginia}, Samuel[2], Samuel[1] {of Ireland}, James[1a] {of
   Bantry Bay, Kenmore, Ireland}, Antoine Dessaure
   Perronett[2a] {Crocketagni of Montauban, France},
   Gabriel Gustave[3a] {of Bourdeau, France}, William
   Jaques[4a] {de Crocketagni of Garonne, France},
   Gustave Matthew[5a], Robert Wade Edbert[6a]]

Crockett of South Carolina. His mother was Lucinda[4] [Francis[3], Jacob[2] {of Wilkes County, Georgia}, Thomas[1] {of Rossshire, Logan, Scotland}] McLendon of Jasper, Pickens County, Georgia. Susan Jane and George[5] had seven children:

a. Eugenia Mindora[6] "Minnie" Crockett
born on April 24, 1868 at Cross Keys, DeKalb County, Georgia. Her date and place of death is not known. She married Leroy Yoman Carter [afa Leroy G. Darter]. The date and place of their marriage is not known. He was born on August 30, 1868 in South Carolina. He died on August 27, 1955 in Los Angeles, Los Angeles County, California. His father was Jasper McClellan W. C. [William, Thomas] Carter of Walterboro, Colleton County, South Carolina. His mother was Minnoa "Minnie" Charleston of Orangeburg County, South Carolina. Issue, if any, is not known.

b. William J.[6] Crockett
born on January 1, 1870 at Cross Keys, DeKalb County, Georgia. His date and place of death is not known.

c. John Clark[6] Crockett
born circa 1872 at Cross Keys, DeKalb County, Georgia. He died, age 72, on October 18, 1944 in

Fulton County, Georgia. He married Mary W. (Unknown). She was born circa 1880 in Georgia. Her father and mother were born in South Carolina. Issue, if any, is not known.

d. James Hunter[6] Crockett
    [Editor's Note: Sometimes found as Jefferson H., they are one in the same person]
    born on September 22, 1876 at Cross Keys, DeKalb County, Georgia. He died on September 22, 1941 at Los Angeles [city of], California. He married Ethel E. (Unknown) in 1898 in Georgia. She was born in 1879 in the Province of Ontario, Canada. Her date and place of death is not known. In 1910 the family was living at Detroit, Wayne County, Michigan. By 1930 they were divorced, as James[4] appears then on the U. S. Census living in Los Angeles [city of], California with his brother-in-law and sister, Leroy Yoman Carter and Minnie[4] Crockett Carter]. James[6] and Ethel had at least two children: Thaddeus[7] and Myrtle[7].

e. Franklin Alondo[6] Crockett
    born on August 24, 1879 at Cross Keys, DeKalb County, Georgia. He died on January 19, 1954 at Los Angeles [city of], California and was interred there on January 25, 1954 in the Los Angeles National Cemetery [Section 25, Row E,

Site 16]. He married Flora (Unknown). He was a private in the U. S. Army during the Spanish-American War.

f. Robert Samuel[6] Crockett
born on April 2, 1883, either in DeKalb County or Fulton County, Georgia. He died on December 12, 1948 at Sacramento, Sacramento County, California. He married Mary (Unknown).

g. Susan O'Dell[6] Crockett
born on February 24, 1885 at Atlanta, Fulton County, Georgia. She died on May 20, 1970 at Los Angeles [city of], California. She married George David Green on April 5, 1907 at Los Angeles [city of], California. He was born on January 9, 1888 at Louisville, Jefferson County, Kentucky. He died on May 12, 1919 at Los Angeles [city of], California. His father was Charles F. Green of Louisville, Jefferson County, Kentucky. His mother was Lucinda Belle [Robert D.] Willis of Kentucky. Susan and George had ten children: Ronald Carroll, Maggie, Phillis Louise [a twin], Willis [a twin], George David, Virginia Elizabeth [another record calls her Virginia Raburn], Frederick Charles "Fred" [who died an infant], Herbert Harry, Frederick William and Susan Jane [Editor's Note: another researcher says Susan

O'Dell[6] married, second, David Passow and had three children: Lorraine, Richard and Dwain].

[EDITOR'S NOTE: There may have been three other children who died in infancy]

7. Laura L. (Zeleakia) Osmore
born on April 29, 1848 in DeKalb County, Georgia. She died, age 54, on July 13, 1903 in Tennessee [although another researcher says possibly Tennessee]. She married, first, James Virgil[5] Hood on February 29, 1872 in DeKalb County, Georgia. He was born on August 8, 1849 in Georgia. He died on December 16, 1873 in Georgia and was buried in the Wesley Chapel Methodist Churchyard Cemetery in DeKalb County, Georgia. His father was Samuel Oliver Hazard[4] [James[3] {of Lancaster County, South Carolina}, Allen[2], William[1] {of Scotland}] Hood of Five Forks, Gwinnett County, Georgia and later of Sherman County, Texas. His mother was Mary Ann [John {of Spartanburg County, South Carolina}] Bankston of Gwinnett County, Georgia. Laura and James[5] had a child:

a. Mary Liza[6] Hood
born circa 1872 in DeKalb County, Georgia. Her date and place of death is not known. In 1880, at age 8, she lived with her parents.

Laura married, second, Robert Sandford Conley. They were married sometime after 1873 [the date of her first husband's death] and before 1882 [the date of their first child] in Georgia. Robert was born on May 7, 1834 in Georgia. He died on January 18, 1896 at Lyerly, Chattooga County, Georgia. His father was William [Patrick] Conley of South Carolina. His mother was Rebecca G. Storey [Robert {of Halifax County, Virginia}] Wood of Spartenburg County, South Carolina. Laura and Robert had four children:

b. Mable "Mattie" Conley
born on February 5, 1882 in Georgia. She died in January 1974 at Chattanooga, Hamilton County, Tennessee. She married James R. Crowe circa 1911/1912 at Chattanooga, Hamilton County, Tennessee. He was born on April 27, 1881 in Georgia. He died on November 19, 1935 at Chattanooga, Hamilton County, Tennessee and was buried on November 21, 1935 at Lyerly, Chatooga County, Georgia. His father was John B. Crowe of Georgia. His mother was Amanda Powers of Georgia. Mattie and James had one child: Laura Lee.

c. Katherine "Katie" Conley
born on May 28, 1884 in Georgia. She died on June 2, 1969 in Alabama. She married Alfred

Russell West, probably circa 1914/1915 in Chattanooga, Hamilton County, Tennessee. He was born on June 12, 1882 in Tennessee. He died on March 19, 1965 in Bridgeport County, Alabama. His father was Silas Mercer [Simpson, John Bakeman, John] West of Sinking Cove, Franklin County, Tennessee. His mother was Martha Jane [John {of North Carolina}, William] Holder of Alabama. Katherine and Alfred had three children: Virginia Mae, (infant/a twin who lived only one day) and Olive R. "Polly" [a twin].

Alfred had married, first, Martha J. (Unknown) of Tennessee, sometime before 1883 [when their first child was born] in Tennessee. She was born circa 1856 in Tennessee. Her date and place of death is not known. Alfred and Martha had three children: Alfred K., Lena and James S.

d. Robert Willis Conley
born on August 3, 1886 in Lyerly, Chattooga County, Georgia. He died on December 29, 1906 in Walker County, Georgia.

e. Annie Laura Conley
born in 1890 in Georgia. She died on January 25, 1979 in Pulaski County, Kentucky. She married Claude E. Avera circa 1906/1907, probably in

Georgia. He was born on September 7, 1882 in Georgia. He died on January 4, 1966 at Somerset, Pulaski County, Kentucky. His father was "Doctor" William Alexander [William Alexander {of Warren County, Georgia}, "Doctor" Alexander] Avera of Stepleton, Jefferson County, Georgia. His mother was Anna Judson [Wiley Thomas {of Wilkes County, Georgia}, Joseph] Holmes of Georgia. Annie and Claude had four children: Robert A., Ruth, Nell W. and Edith.

8. Jefferson Gadwell Osmore

born on September 26, 1851 at Clarkston, DeKalb County, Georgia. He died on November 8 [or the 11th], 1939 at Fairburn, Fulton County, Georgia and was buried in the Wesley Chapel Methodist Church Cemetery in DeKalb County, Georgia. He married, first, Ella Jane Hunter on November 9, 1877, probably at Fairburn, Fulton County, Georgia. Ella was born on February 13, 1858 in DeKalb County, Georgia. She died on November 3, 1901 at DeKalb County, Georgia and was buried there in the Wesley Chapel Methodist Church Cemetery. Her father was LeRoy G. [Ferisa] Hunter of Evans, DeKalb County, Georgia. Her mother was Susan M. [Joseph D. {of South Carolina}] Langford of North Carolina. Jefferson and Ella Jane had five children: Hattie Lee, Windsor Wilkerson "Jack," Sally Sue, Amis Grace

85

"Allie" and Robert LeRoy "Roy."

Jefferson married, second, his niece, Pamelia Elizabeth [afa Permelia] Ozmer. The date and place of their marriage is not known. Pamelia was born on May 16, 1859, presumably in Georgia. She died on July 6, 1931 [another record says she died on November 3, 1931] in DeKalb County, Georgia and was buried in the Wesley Chapel Methodist Church Cemetery in DeKalb County, Georgia. Her father was John Windsor [Robert Clark, Richard {of Brunswick County, Virginia}, (William)] Osmore of Henry County [later DeKalb County], North Carolina [Editor's Note: this was Jefferson Gadwell's brother]. Her mother was Elizabeth Parr[5] [William[4] {of North Carolina and later of Georgia}, John[3], Thomas[2] {of Sussex County, Virginia}, William[1] {of London, England}] Mitchell of DeKalb County, Georgia. There was no issue.

9. Alfred Clark "Scott" Osmore
born on November 27, 1855 in DeKalb County, Georgia. He died in April 1920 at Newcastle, Young County, Texas. He married Inez Alzada[8] Hunt on November 7, 1880 in Georgia. Inez[8] was born on August 26, 1861 at Thomaston, Upson County, Georgia. She died on May 12, 1908 at Colorado City, Mitchell County, Texas. Her father was "Doctor" James Oliver[7] [Thomas[6], Turner[5] {of

86

Dinwiddie County, Virginia}, John[4] {of Sussex County, Virginia}, Thomas[3] {of Charles City, Charles County, Virginia}, William[2] {of Isle of Wight County, Virginia}, William[1] {of England}]] Hunt {born 1835, a physician} of Georgia. His mother was Alzada Frances Rowe {born 1835} of Whitesville, Harris County, Georgia. Inez once said in a letter to her sister in East Texas, "The Ozmer folks [referring to her inlaws, Robert Clark and Elizabeth Graham Ozmer] were mean," which may explain why in 1894 they moved to Texas. Alfred and Inez[8] had at least one child:

a. Carlton Hunt Ozmer
    born on December 14, 1881 Chattooga County, Georgia. He died on March 8, 1971 at Dallas [city of], Texas [another researcher says Newcastle, Young County, Texas—he may have lived there and died in a Dallas facility]. He married Fannie Leona Stringer on August 8 [another record says March 9th], 1906 at True Community, Young County, Texas. She was born on March 16, 1885 at True Community, Young County, Texas. She died on February 15, 1945 at True Community, Young County, Texas. Her father was Sanders M. [Simon, Simon {of Edgecomb County, North Carolina}, Charles] Stringer of Lawrence County, Mississippi. Her mother was Nanny A. Hardy of

Kentucky. Carlton and Fannie had five children: Thomas Wilford "Bill," Lucille, Robert, Fannie Inez and Johnny Carlton.

10. Robert Osmore
   born on August 19, 1858 in DeKalb County, Georgia. He died, along with his mother, just prior to his eleventh birthday, after being stuck by lightning on August 5, 1869 in DeKalb County, Georgia and is buried there in the Wesley Chapel Methodist Cemetery.

The Life and Times of Richard Osmore

PATERNAL ANCESTRY: [OSMORE: (William)]

MATERNAL ANCESTRY: [(UNKNOWN)]

RICHARD Osmore [also found as Ozmore and Ozmar] was probably born circa 1770/1775, most likely in Dinwiddie County, Virginia. He apparently died circa 1819 [either just before or just after his last child Permelia was born] in Brunswick County, Virginia. [Editor's Note: On the U. S. Census of 1820, his wife, Susan, is listed as the head of household]. His father was probably William Osmore of Dinwiddie and later Greensville County, Virginia. The name of his mother is not known.

[EDITOR'S NOTE: It is probable that William Osmore was Richard's father. In the 1700s, there were only two other male Osmores in the tri-counties of Dinwiddie, Brunswick and Greensville, born circa the 1750s/1760s, namely John and William {presumably brothers}. Since all of John's children have been accounted for, it seems that William is the logical choice for this Richard's father. It is also interesting to note that John Osmore also had a child named Richard.]

RICHARD married Susanna "Susan" Wade based on a marriage bond on November 25, 1799 between Richard Osmore and Susan Wade, age 21, in Brunswick County, Virginia. Thomas Wade was the Surety. David Elder and Edward Taylor were the Witnesses. They were married by Justice of the Peace, William McConnalls.

RICHARD of Brunswick County, Virginia had an indenture awarded against him as recorded in September 1818 [Deed Book 24, Page 105] by John P. Malone in the amount of $93.90 for Malone's "faithful performance of his duties as Port Master at Westward Mill, Virginia during the years of 1816 and 1817 [Editor's Note: The Westward Mill was a grist mill located on the Meherrin River in Brunswick County]. The debt was secured by the following personal property of Richard Osmore: . . . goods and chattels, 6 head of cattle, 3 feather beds & furniture & bedstead, 1 bay mare, one gun, one chest, one table, iron potts, 2 ovens, 2 skillets, 6 plates, 6 knives & forks, two dishes, a set of cups & saucers, 19 head of hogs & all the plantation. According to the indenture, Malone would permit Ozmore to remain in pos- session of his property until December [1818] when, if not paid, they would be sold to the highest bidder to pay the debts. The original complaint was dated and acknowledged by Osmar [Osmore] on the 21st of February 1818 and heard in the Brunswick County

Court on June 22, 1818.

[EDITOR'S NOTE: The story that unfolds here is that Richard Osmore, for whatever reason {crop failure due to weather, pests, etc.} found himself in debt to the grist mill for grinding his crop and, when he was unable to pay them, they attached all of his possessions. Although there is no remaining record found of the final disposition, apparently he was unable to pay and lost everything. This seems obvious, because by 1920 he apparently was deceased and, sometime after the 1920 U. S. Census, his widow Susan took her children south to Georgia to start a new life. It makes one wonder if Richard became so despondent over these unfortunate events that he either became ill and died, or possibly even took his own life. To make matters worse, Susan was pregnant with their last child the very month the debt was due.]

Susan Wade was born circa 1778, probably in either Greensville, Dinwiddie or Brunswick County, Virginia. She died sometime after 1860 where, at age 88, she was living at Unionville, Monroe County, Georgia. Her father may have been Edward[5] [Robert[4], Andrew[3], Edward[2] II, Edward[1] {of London, England}]] Wade of Greensville County {born January 29, 1749 in Halifax County}, Virginia. If so, her mother would have been Letitia[4] " Letty" [Abraham[3], Jean/John[2]

{Martain}, Abraham[1] {of Pale Park, Dorsetshire, England}, John[1a]] Martin of Charlotte County, Virginia [Editor's Note: Edward[5] and Letitia[4] were married on October 15, 1768 in James City County, Virginia].

[EDITOR'S NOTE: Many researchers, including the Church of Latter Day Saints database, record Susan Wade as marrying a George Osmore; however, no actual record of this marriage has been found and is deemed erroneous.]

Mrs. Susan Osmoore [age 26-45] appeared on the 1820 U.S. Census for Meherrin Parish, Brunswick County, Virginia as the head of the household, along with 2 males [under age 10], 1 male [age 10-16], 1 male [age 16-18], 1 male [age 18-26], 3 females [under age 10], 2 females [age 10-16], and 2 females [age 16-26] [Editor's Note: All together there were twelve people living in the household; so, whether there were other children of Richard and Susan who are not recorded here, or other extended family living with her, it is not known].

Susan and her children removed to Morgan County, Georgia sometime between 1820 and 1830. She appears on the 1830 U.S. Census for Morgan County, Georgia as Susan Osmore [age 50-60], along with 2 males [age 10-15], 1 male [age 20-30], 1 female [age

10-15], and 2 females [age 15-20].

Susan Wade Osmer drew lot #3, 26th District, 2nd Section, Cherokee County, [now Murray and Gilmer Counties], Georgia in the 1932 Cherokee Lottery.

Susan's children drew land in the 1832 Cherokee Land Lottery, drawing Land Lot #214, 8th District, 4th Section in Morgan County [which became Walker County], Georgia.

Susan Ozmore, age 72, appears on the 1850 U. S. Census for Monroe County, Georgia in the household of H. C. Thornton, age 30, Martha [Susan's grand-daughter and daughter of Eliza Osmore and Jonathan Ball], age 25, two daughters, Francie, age 3, and Eliza J, age 2. There were no slaves listed in her household.

Susan last appears on the 1860 U. S. Census for the Unionville District of Monroe County, Georgia, age 88, born 1771 in Virginia, in the household of Jonathan Ball, husband of her daughter, Eliza.

[EDITOR'S NOTE: Even though Susan's recorded age varies from the 1850 to the 1860 U. S. Census, this is not uncommon, depending on who the census taker got the information from.]

The Children of
Richard Osmore
and Susan Wade

1. Eliza Osmore
   born circa 1802 in Brunswick County, Virginia. She
   died sometime after 1870, probably in Monroe
   County, Georgia. She married Jonathan Ball circa
   1831, probably in Monroe County, Georgia.
   Jonathan was born circa 1799 in Monroe County,
   Georgia. He died sometime before 1870 in Monroe
   County, Georgia [Editor's Note: the 1870 U. S.
   Census for Monroe County, Georgia list Eliza Ball,
   age 69, widow—no one else was listed in the
   household]. The name of his father is not known.
   His mother was Esther (Unknown) [Editor's Note:
   Jonathan Ball is mentioned in the will of William
   Ball dated 19 October 1816 and sworn to on
   January 6, 1817, as the son of Esther Ball]. On the
   1860 U. S. Census for Unionville, Monroe County,
   Georgia, Eliza, age 35, appears with her husband,
   Jonathan Ball, age 61, daughter Adaline, age 18,
   and Susan Osmore, age 88, Eliza's mother. Eliza
   and Jonathan had eight children:

   a. Martha O. Ball
      born on August 22, 1824 in Monroe County,
      Georgia. She died on October 26, 1893 at High
      Falls, Monroe County, Georgia and was buried

there in the Providence Church Cemetery at High Falls. She married Hampton Cordus[8] Thornton on November 26, 1846 in Monroe County, Georgia. He was born on November 25, 1820 in Jasper County, Georgia. He died on October 27, 1875 in Monroe County, Georgia and was buried in the Providence Church Cemetery at High Falls. Hampton[8]'s father was Cullen[7] [Richard[6] {of Johnson County, North Carolina}, Herod[5] {of Virginia}, Thomas[4] {of Farnham, Richmond, Virginia}, Mark I.[3], Luke[2], William[1] {of Yorkshire, England}, William[1a], Francis[2a], Robert[3a], William[4a], Robert[5a], Robert[6a], Robert[7a], Thomas[8a], William[9a], John[10a] {surname deThornton, born circa 1260}, William[11a], "Sir" Robert[12a] {born circa 1189}] Thornton of Oglethorp County, Georgia. His mother was Mary[5] "Polly" [John[4] {of Hanover County, Virginia}, Thomas[3], Thomas[2], William[1] {of Corle Castle, England and later of Stephens, King and Queen County, Virginia}] Banks of Monroe County, Georgia. Issue, if any, is not known.

b. Anna Eliza Ball
born on December 27, 1827 in Georgia. She died circa 1887 at Unionville, Monroe County, Georgia and was buried in the Pleasant Hill Methodist Church Cemetery in Lamar County, Georgia. She married Robert Henry Brown on

February 28, 1849 in Monroe County, Georgia. He was born on June 3, 1824 in Lincoln County, Georgia. He died on March 11, 1917 in Claiborne Parish, Louisiana and was buried in the Salem Methodist Church Cemetery in Lincoln Parish, Louisiana. The name of his father and mother is not known. Anna and Robert had six children: Joe Wesley, Jonathan L., Lucinda F., Martha Ann, Nancy J. and William R.

c. Sarah Elizabeth Ball

born circa 1830 in Monroe County, Georgia. She died on December 3, 1895 in Newton County, Mississippi and was buried there in the Crossroads Baptist Church Cemetery. Sarah married Richard Columbus[8] Thornton on October 2, 1845 in Monroe County, Georgia. He was born circa 1819 in Jasper County, Georgia. He died on February 1, 1882 in Newton County, Mississippi and was buried there in the Crossroads Baptist Church Cemetery. His father was Cullen[7] [Richard[6] {of Johnson County, North Carolina}, Herod[5] {of Virginia}, Thomas[4] {of Farnham, Richmond, Virginia}, Mark I.[3], Luke[2], William[1] {of Yorkshire, England}, William[1a], Francis[2a], Robert[3a], William[4a], Robert[5a], Robert[6a], Robert[7a], Thomas[8a], William[9a], John[10a] {deThornton, born circa 1260},

William[11a], "Sir" Robert[12a] {born circa 1189}] Thornton of Oglethorp County, Georgia. His mother was Mary "Polly" [John {of Hanover County, Virginia}, Thomas] Banks of Monroe County, Georgia. Sarah and Richard[8] had eight children: William Cordius[9], Mary Ann[9], Sarah Lavina[9] "Viney," Frances Lucinda[9], Henry B.[9], Richard Joseph[9], Absalom Jones[9] and John Wethersby[9].

d. Joel O. Ball

born circa 1832 in Monroe County, Georgia. He died sometime between 1870 [when he last appears on the U. S. Census] and 1880, possibly in Collin County or Hill County, Texas. He married Mary A. (Unknown) sometime before 1855. She was born circa 1834 in Georgia. Her date and place of death is not known. Joel and Mary had five children: Charles Rufus, Emma, Jonathan W., Robert J. and William.

e. Jonathan W. Ball

born on January 11, 1834 in Monroe County, Georgia. He died on February 2, 1879 in Monroe County, Georgia and was buried in the Pleasant Hill Methodist Church Cemetery in Lamar County, Georgia. He married Mary Jane Barkley on December 31, 1857 in Monroe County, Georgia. She was born on February 16,

1839 in Monroe County, Georgia. She died on December 30, 1919 in Monroe County, Georgia and was buried in the Pleasant Hill Methodist Church Cemetery in Lamar County, Georgia. The name of her father and mother is not known. Jonathan and Mary Jane had seven children: Alice G., Charlie Christopher, Emma W., James Wiley, Lovick P., Mary E. and Robert Lee.

f. Susan Frances Ball
    born on February 5, 1836 in Monroe County, Georgia. She died on August 20, 1926 in Lamar County, Georgia and was buried there in the Pleasant Hill Methodist Church Cemetery. She married William Leven Pritchett on December 18, 1856 in Monroe County, Georgia. He was born circa 1838, presumably in Hancock County [but possibly Monroe County], Georgia. He died, age 24, of measles on June 19, 1862 near Richmond [city of], Virginia during the U. S. Civil War [he had enlisted with the C.S.A. as a private on March 4, 1862]. His father was William Leven [Joseph Phillip {of Beaufort County, North Carolina}, Phillip] Pritchett of Hancock County, Georgia. His mother was Eveline {afa Evelina} [John of North Carolina}, William] Burgay [afa Bagley] of Monroe County, Georgia. Susan and William had five

children: Joel, Lucinda, Robert F., Susan Frances and Jonathan Leven.

g. Robert F. Ball
born circa 1840 in Georgia. He died, age 22, on August 12, 1862 in an army camp near Richmond [city of], Virginia.

h. Lucinda Adeline Ball
born circa 1842 in Georgia. Her date and place of death is not known.

2. **Robert Clark Osmore**
born circa 1810 in Brunswick County, Virginia. He died on April 25, 1858 in DeKalb County, Georgia. He married Elizabeth[4] Graham circa 1831/1832, presumably in Henry County [which later became DeKalb County], Georgia. Elizabeth[4] was born in 1812 in North Carolina. She died on August 5, 1869 in DeKalb County, Georgia and was buried there in the Wesley Chapel Methodist Church Cemetery. Her father was Robert Windsor[3] [William Grimes[2], George[1] {of Scotland}, John[1a] {a schoolmaster of County Down, Ireland}] Graham of Richmond County, North Carolina and later of McDonough, Henry County, Georgia. Her mother was Chrissie[3] "Kiddy" [Joshua[2] {of Brunswick County, Virginia and later of the Marlboro District of South Carolina}, John George[1] {of Switzerland, and later

of Weurttenburg, Germany}, Jacob[1a] {known as Amon of Zurich, Switzerland}, Jorle[2a] {Ammann}] Ammons of the Marlborough District of South Carolina. Robert and Elizabeth[4] had ten children: Martha Ann, John Windsor, Mary Elizabeth, Sarah Caroline, George Smith, Susan Jane, Laura (Zeleakia), Jefferson Gadwell, Alfred Clark "Scott" and Robert.

3. **Thomas Osmore** [afa Ozmore]
born circa 1812 in Virginia. He died sometime after 1880, presumably in Georgia. He married Keziah Shinly on December 21, 1836 in Randolph County, Georgia. Her date and place of birth and death is not known. The name of her father and mother is not known. Thomas and Keziah had two children:

a. Martha Alberta Osmore
born on April 25, 1938 in Randolph County, Georgia. She died, age 70, on April 18, 1909 in Clay County, Georgia. She married Dennis W. DeLacy on May 4, 1859 in Randolph County, Georgia. He was born in 1828 in Georgia [circa 1853/1855 he was living at Greenville, Meriweather County, Georgia; another researcher says he was born in Ireland]. He died on November 13, 1867 in Randolph County, Georgia. The name of his father and mother is not known. Martha and Dennis had three

children: Mary Denise "Molly," Emmett Zulene and Mattie.

Martha married, second, Robert Weakley Duke on August 15, 1869 in Randolph County, Georgia. He was born on August 27, 1844 in Butts County, Georgia. He died on October 29, 1932 in Early County, Georgia. His father was William Marshall [Henry M., Taylor {of Lunenburg, Lunenburg County, Virginia}, James {born in 1730; married Mary Byrd, of Charles City, Charles County, Virginia}] Duke of Morgan County, Georgia [who, as a Confederate soldier during the U.S. Civil War, died on March 5, 1865 at Florence, Florence County, South Carolina]. His mother was Nancy Clementine Wilkerson of Morgan County, Georgia. Martha and Robert had five children: Sallie Alberta, William, Edward D., Robert and Charles Franklin "Charlie."

b. John Ozmore
born in 1847 in Randolph County, Georgia. His date and place of death is not known.

Thomas married, second, Piercy Ann[6] [afa Puria] Thompson on August 27, 1857 in Randolph County, Georgia. She was born on July 30, 1830 in Wayne County, North Carolina. She died on

February 4, 1892 in Randolph County, Georgia. Her father was Jeremiah[5] [Charles[4] {of Dinwiddie County, Virginia}, William[3] {of Surry County, Virginia}, William[2] {of Essex County, Virginia}, William[1] {of Winwick, Lancashire, England}, William[1a], William[2a] {of Leigh, Wiltshire, England}, Henry[3a] {of Lenham, Kent, England}, Thomas[4a] {of Sandwich, Kent, England}, Thomas[5a] {born circa 1519}] Thompson of Wayne County, North Carolina. Her mother was Mary Angelina (Unknown) of South Carolina and later of Wayne County, North Carolina. Thomas and Piercy[6] had five children:

b. Cordelia V. Ozmore
    born on October 17, 1858 in Randolph County, Georgia. She died on June 25, 1917 in Randolph County, Georgia. She married James M. Jordan on May 17, 1893 in Bibb County, Georgia. He was born circa 1852 in Georgia. His date and place of death is not known. The name of his father and mother is not known. Cordelia and James had a child: John.

c. Walter T. Ozmore
    born on February 10, 1862 in Randolph County, Georgia. He died in 1952 at Lakeland, Polk County, Florida. He married Ella Tabulla[5] Corum on June 3, 1885, probably in Randolph

County, Georgia. She was born on December 25, 1861 in Randolph County, Georgia. She died on December 17, 1939 in Polk County, Florida. Her father was George Washington[4] [Thomas[3] {of Wilkes County, Georgia}, William[2] {of Fauquier County, Virginia}, William S.[1] {of Culmstock, Devonshire, England}]] Corum of Benevalance, Randolph County, Georgia. Her mother was Susannah Manor of Sparks, Cook County, Georgia. Walter and Ella[5] had two children: Raymond Leonard and Flora Inez.

d. Frances Isabelle Ozmore
born on December 21, 1864 in Randolph County, Georgia. She died on December 4, 1957 in Randolph County, Georgia. She married Walter Scott Hester in 1883 in Randolph County, Georgia. He was born on August 4, 1857 in Randolph County, Georgia. He died on October 6, 1917 at Cuthbert, Randolph County, Georgia. His father was Robert B. [William B. {of Kershaw County, South Carolina}, Zachariah, William F.] Hester of Cowetta County, Georgia. His mother was Sarah Louisa[9] [Zachary[8] {of North Carolina}, Levi[7] {of New Bern, Craven County, North Carolina}, "Captain" Edward[6], John[5], John Mitchell[4], Edward[3] {of Isle of Wight County, Virginia}, William[2] {of Nansemond County, Virginia}, John[1] {of Cuck-

field, Sussex, England}] Gatlin of Cowetta County, Georgia. Frances and Walter had five children: Elmore "Elmo" Cleveland, Mabel, Ruth, John [who died an infant] and Ross E.

e. Willie H. Ozmore
born on October 19, 1869 at Randolph County, Georgia. Her date and place of death is not known.

4. George F. Osmore
born on March 22, 1817 in Brunswick County, Virginia. He died on July 19, 1894 at Magnolia, Columbia County, Arkansas. He married Nancy Elizabeth Bray on January 6, 1844 in Monroe County, Georgia. She was born on October 18, 1819 in Georgia. She died on May 28, 1897 at Magnolia, Columbia County, Arkansas. The name of her father and mother is not known [her father was from Georgia and her mother from South Carolina]. George and his family removed to Arkansas in 1859. He enlisted as a private in the Confederate Army on May 8, 1862. His descendants still reside in Arkansas and Texas [as of 1986]. George and Nancy had five children:

a. William F. Ozmer
born on October 14, 1844 in Monroe County, Georgia. He died on September 12, 1863,

possibly at Magnolia, Columbia County, Arkansas.

b. George R. Ozmer
born on October 20, 1846 in Monroe County, Georgia. He died on January 29, 1860 in Monroe County, Georgia.

c. Mary E. Ozmer
born on March 31, 1849 in Monroe County, Georgia. Her date and place of death is not known.

d. Henry Augustus Ozmer
born on August 9, 1851 in Monroe County, Georgia. He died on June 15, 1941 at Magnolia, Columbia County, Arkansas. He married Virginia Peck Faulk on October 1, 1873 in Columbia County, Arkansas. She was born on February 5, 1953 at Magnolia, Columbia County, Arkansas. She died on May 5, 1941 at Magnolia, Columbia County, Arkansas. Her father was William F. [John {of North Carolina}] Faulk of Columbia County, Georgia and later of Twiggs County, Georgia. Her mother was Sarah Caroline [Harrison Whitfield {of Georgia and later of Alabama}, Daniel B. {of North Carolina}] Lewis of Eufaula, Barbour County, Alabama. Henry and Virginia had six children:

Henry Faulk, Alie P., Virginia Ollie., Herman Augusta, Nancy Lee and Mary Floyd.

e. (child) Ozmer
born on July 23, 1855 in Monroe County, Georgia. The child died, age 5 days, on July 28, 1855 in Monroe County, Georgia.

5. Permelia J. [afa Pamelia] Ozmore
born on August 19, 1819 in Brunswick County, Virginia. She died on November 23, 1873 in Pike County, Georgia. She married William Harper[4] Graham on February 14, 1837 in Monroe County, Georgia [another researcher says Forsyth County, Georgia]. He was born in 1819 in Georgia. He died in 1870 in Monroe County, Georgia. His father was "Reverend" Robert Windsor[3] [William Grimes[2], George[1] {of Scotland}, John[1a] {a schoolmaster of County Down, Ireland}] Graham of Richmond County, North Carolina and later of McDonough, Henry County, Georgia. Her mother was Chrissie[3] "Kiddy" [Joshua[2] {of Brunswick County, Virginia and later of the Marlboro District of South Carolina}, John George[1] {of Switzerland, and later of Weurttenburg, Germany}, Jacob[1a] {known as Amon of Zurich, Switzerland}, Jorle[2a] {Ammann}] Ammons of the Marlborough District of South Carolina. Pamelia and William[4] had twelve children:

a. George A.[5] Graham
born in 1837 in Monroe County, Georgia. He died in 1863 in the area of Atlanta, Fulton County, Georgia while defending the city during the U. S. Civil War. He married Elizabeth Florida[8] Beckham on December 22, 1858 in Georgia. She was born on May 27, 1834 in Pike County, Georgia. She died on April 26, 1885 in Georgia. Her father was Absalom Butler[7] [Laban[6], Simon[5] {of Hanover County, Virginia}, William[4] {of Spotsylvania, Essex County, Virginia}, William[3] {of Creke, Norfolk County, Virginia}, Simon[2], William[1] {of East Beckam, County Norfolk, England}] Beckham of Pike County, Georgia. His mother was Susan Gilbert of Pike County, Georgia. George[5] and Elizabeth[8] had two children: William A.[6] and Georgianne[6].

b. John Philip[5] Graham
born in 1839 in Monroe County, Georgia. He died of smallpox in a Union prison in 1863 at Rock Island, Rock Island County, Illinois during the U. S. Civil War. He married Susan Frances[7] Story on October 25, 1859 in Pike County, Georgia. She was born on August 26, 1838 in Pike County, Georgia. She died on May 12, 1929 in Pike County, Georgia. Her father was James Wiley[6] [William[5], James Obediah[4], James[3] {of

Richmond, Wise County, Virginia}, James[2], Edward[1] {of Portslade, Sussex, England}] Story of Mecklinburg County, North Carolina. Her mother was Rebecca[8] [Daniel[7] {of Edgefield, Edgefield County, South Carolina}, Russell[6] {of Granville County, North Carolina}, Thomas[5] {of Hanover County, Virginia}, William[4] {of Spotsylvania, Essex County, Virginia}, William[3] {of Creke, Norfolk County, Virginia}, Simon[2], William[1] {of East Beckham, County Norfolk, England}] Beckham of Washington County, Georgia. There was no issue.

Susan married, second, Hugh Henry Reeves in 1865 in Pike County, Georgia. He was born in April 1838 in Pike County, Georgia. He died on April 3, 1904 at Molena, Pike County, Georgia. The name of his father and mother is not known. Susan and Hugh had seven children: Martha Emma "Mattie," Frances R. "Fannie," Etta Lavina, George Andrew, Willie Perlina, Sallie E. and Avie D.

c. William R.[5] Graham
born in 1842 at Division, Monroe County, Georgia. He died in 1919 in Baldwin County, Georgia.

d. James Windsor[5] Graham
born on January 9, 1844 at Division, Monroe County, Georgia. He died on October 19, 1915, probably at Lindale, Floyd County, Georgia. He married Mary Emma Lawrence on August 21, 1873 in Pike County, Georgia. She was born in August 1858 in Georgia. She died in 1935 in Georgia. The name of her father and mother is not known. James[5] and Mary had nine children: Clyde E.[6], Sally[6], Benjamin Gordon[6], Fannie Lee[6], Martha L.[6], Grover Cleveland[6], Annett[6], William Oliver[6] and Jewell Winger[6].

e. Moses Absolem[5] Graham
born in 1846 at Division, Monroe County, Georgia. His date and place of death is not known. He married Louisa Frances Patterson on August 15, 1863 in Meriweather County, Georgia. She was born on July 29, 1846 in Georgia. She died on October 20, 1933 in Forsyth County, Georgia. Her father was Robert Patterson of Caroll County, Georgia. Her mother was Emeline[5] [Wenlock C.[4] {of Wayne County, North Carolina}, Christopher[3] {of Perquimans County, North Carolina}, Peter[2], Peter[1] {of Dean Parish, Ullock, Cumberland County, England}, Christopher[1a], John[2a], John[3a], Cuthbert[4a] {of Egglescliffe, County Durham, England}, Robert[5a] {Peyrson born circa 1519}]

Pearson of Carroll County, Georgia. On the 1880 U. S. Census, the family was living at Cave Spring, Floyd County, Georgia [also living with them was Moses[5]'s brother, Patrick H.[5] Graham, age 20]. Moses[5] and Louisa had seven children: Florida Indiana[6], Permalia Emeline[6], Sarah Elizabeth[6], Mirandae Lenora[6], Marvin Pierce[6], Bascom Pain[6] and William Robert[6].

f. Susan Adaline[5] Graham
born in 1848 at Division, Monroe County, Georgia. Her date and place of death is not known.

g. Jeremiah Fleming[5] Graham
born in July 1850 at Division, Monroe County, Georgia. He died in 1917 in Pike County, Georgia. He married Anna Narcissa Purdue circa 1872, presumably in Pike County, Georgia. She was born in April 1852 in Georgia. She died in 1918 in Pike County, Georgia and was buried in the Greenwood Cemetery at Barnesville, Lamar County, Georgia. The name of her father and mother is not known. Jeremiah[5] and Anna had two children: Willie C.[6] and Walter H.[6].

h. Martha Caroline[5] Graham
born on June 5, 1852 in Monroe County, Georgia. She died on June 8, 1925 in Union

County, Georgia. She married Newsome Asbury[8] Sappington on July 21, 1872 in Monroe County, Georgia. He was born on March 4, 1837 in Oglethorpe County, Georgia. He died on February 18, 1915 in Lamar County, Georgia. His father was Henry T.[5] [Richard[4] {of Anne Arundel County, Maryland}, John[3], Jr., John[2] {of Cecil County, Maryland}, Nathaniel[1] {of Wales}] Sappington of Oglethorpe County, Georgia. His mother was Sarah Smith[7] [John Hardeman[6] {of Brunswick County, Virginia}, Glen Appleton[5] {Henrico County, Virginia}, Thomas[4] {Goochland County, Virginia}, John[3] {of Henrico County, Virginia}, Thomas[2] {of Southwarke Parish, Surry County, Virginia}, William[1] {born circa 1635 of Dolsereau, Mereionetshire, Wales}, Humphrey[1a]] Owen of Murray County, Georgia. Martha[5] and Newsome[8] had eight children: Harriet Elizabeth[9], Sarah "Sally" Smith[9], Benjamin Pete[9], Thomas Jonas[9], Emmet Patrick[9] "Ernest," Pamelia[9] "Frankie," William Graham[9] and George Newsome[9].

Newsome[8] had married, first, Mary E.[7] "Molly" Coppedge in 1866 in Pike County, Georgia. She was born on January 12, 1845 in Pike County, Georgia. She died on March 30, 1872 in Lamar County, Georgia. Her father was John W.[6] [Charles[5] {of Wicomico, Gloucester County,

Virginia}, Charles[4] {of Northumberland County, Virginia}, William[3], Charles[2], William[1] {of Chelworth, Wilshire, England}] Coppedge of Anson County, North Carolina. Her mother was Eliza Jane[5] [John[4] {of Warren County, Georgia}, Isaiah[3] {of Amherst County, Virginia}, Matthew[2], Francis[1] {of Warwick County, Bermuda}, George[1a] IV {of Milton, Gravesend, Kent, England}, George[2a] III, George[3a] II, George[4a] {of Throwleigh, Devonshire, England}, William[5a]] Tucker of Barnsville, Lamar County, Georgia. Newsome[8] and Mary[7] had one child: Nettie Vorus[9].

I. Sarah Miranda[5] Graham
    born on June 22, 1854 at Division, Monroe County, Georgia. She died on October 15, 1901 in Upson County, Georgia and was buried there in the Antioch United Methodist Church Cemetery. She married Charles Marcus Gordy on December 22, 1875 in Upson County, Georgia. He was born in October 1856 in Georgia. He died on April 29, 1944 in Upson County, Georgia. His father was George W. [Leonard, II {of Hancock County, Georgia}, Leonard {of Worcester County, Maryland}, Peter, Peter {of Lewes, Sussex County, Delaware}] Gordy of Georgia. His mother was Elizabeth[7] [Walter Evans[6] {of North Carolina},

112

Robert[5] {of King and Queen County, Virginia}, George[4], Robert[3], "Captain" Jacob[2], Anthony[1] {of Lincolnshire, England}] Lumpkin of Jasper County, Georgia. Sarah[5] and Charles had nine children: Oscar Clarence, Edgar Patterson, Patricia Naomi, Milton E., Nettie, George W., Emmett Henson, Odie Clemons and Charley Earnest.

j. Mary Frances[5] "Frankie" Graham
born in 1856 in Pike County, Georgia. Her date and place of death is not known.

k. Sophronia C.[5] Graham
born on December 9, 1858 in Upson County, Georgia. She died on June 21, 1897 in Upson County, Georgia. She married Joseph Henry Hoyle on December 14, 1876 [the date was recorded in Joseph Henry Hoyle's bible] in Georgia [Editor's Note: In 1880 they were living at Cave Spring, Floyd County, Georgia]. He was born on July 11, 1856 in Upson County, Georgia. He died on August 12, 1942 in Upson County, Georgia. His father was Francis John Marion [William S. {of Maryland}, John I.] Hoyle of Hancock County, Georgia. His mother was Mary Jane[7] [Walter Evans[6] {of North Carolina}, Robert[5] {of King and Queen County, Virginia}, George[4], Robert[3], "Captain" Jacob[2],

Anthony[1] {of Lincolnshire, England}] Lumpkin of Griffin, Spalding County, Georgia. Sophronia[5] and Joseph had seven children: Mary P., F. P., William Marion, George Benjamin, Josie P., Walter Evans and Henry Harper.

Joseph married, second, Eliza Eason Barker on October 17, 1897 at Thompson, Upson County, Georgia. She was born on May 15, 1862 in Upson County, Georgia. She died on January 25, 1955 in Upson County, Georgia. Her father was Joseph Lewis [John] Barker of Upson County, Georgia. Her mother was Eliza Jane McKinney Johnson of Talbot County, Georgia. Joseph and Eliza had no issue.

1. Patrick H.[5] "Pat" Graham
    born on March 9, 1860 in Georgia. He died on August 20, 1915 in Upson County, Georgia. He married Mary L. "Mamie" Peugh. The date and place of their marriage is unknown. She was born on January 23, 1861 in Upson County, Georgia. She died on September 21, 1928 in Upson County, Georgia. Her father was Robert James [Asa {of Wilkes County, Georgia}, Jehu {of North Carolina}, Jesse {of Guilford, North Carolina}] Peugh of Thomaston, Upson County, Georgia. Her mother was Sarah J. Willingham of Georgia. Issue, if any, is not known.

The Life and Times of
William Osmore

PATERNAL ANCESTRY: [OSMORE: (Unknown)]

MATERNAL ANCESTRY: [(UNKNOWN)]

WILLIAM Osmore [sometimes also found as Ozmar] was probably born circa 1750/1755, probably in Dinwiddie County, Virginia. He died circa 1789 in Greensville County, Virginia, when it was "Ordered that the Overseers of the poor or any one of them to bind out Richard Ozmar [his son] Orphan of (no Christian name given) Ozmar deceased according to Law." The name of his father and mother is not known.

WILLIAM married an unknown wife sometime before circa 1770/1775 [when their child Richard was born], probably in Dinwiddie County, Virginia. Nothing else has been found about this marriage.

[EDITOR'S NOTE: His family may have had a relationship with the Vincent family, as Joseph and Peter Vincent were witnesses at the marriage of his son, William, to Lucy Murrell and, after his death, the son William sued a William Vincent for a debt. The Vincent's may have been from Charles County, Maryland, but no connection of them and the

Osmores are found there.]

WILLIAM first appears on the Dinwiddie County, Virginia Personal Property List on April 10, 1782 as living alone with one Negro under age 16 and three horses.

The Children of
William Osmore
and (Unknown)

1. **Richard Osmore**

   probably born circa 1770/1775, probably in Dinwiddie County [but possibly Greensville County], Virginia. He apparently died by 1920 [either before or after his last child Permelia was born] in Brunswick County, Virginia. [Editor's Note: On the U. S. Census of 1820, his wife, Susan, is listed as the head of household]. He married Susanna "Susan" Wade based on a marriage bond on November 25, 1799 between Richard Osmore and Susan Wade, age 21, in Brunswick County, Virginia. Thomas Wade was the Surety. David Elder and Edward Taylor were the Witnesses. They were married by William McConnalls, Justice of the Peace. Richard and Susan had five children: Eliza, Robert Clark, Thomas, George F. and Permelia J.

[EDITOR'S NOTE: Since William {born circa 1750/ 1755 and died in or before 1789}, it was obviously a son William who married Lucy Murrell]

2. William Osmore
    date of birth, presumably in Dinwiddie County, Virginia is not known. His date of death, presumably in Greensville County, is not known. He married Lucy Murrell on October 17, 1789 [other records say October 13th and October 24th] in Greensville County, Virginia, William Andrews, a Methodist minister, presiding. Joseph Vincent was the bondsman and Peter Vincent, the witness. Lucy's date and place of birth and death is not known. The name of her father and mother is not known.

    William appears on the Greensville County, Virginia Order Book #2 1790-1799, which reads: William Ozmar, plaintiff against William Vincent, defendant, in debt. The case was discontinued at the defendant's costs by agreement of the parties.

    William later appeared on the 1800 Virginia Tax List Index as residing in Greensville County, Virginia in 1798. Issue, if any, is not known.

The Life and Times of
(Unknown) Osmore

PATERNAL ANCESTRY: [OSMORE: (Unknown)]

MATERNAL ANCESTRY: [(UNKNOWN)]

(UNKNOWN) Osmore's date and place of birth [presumably circa 1730] and death is not known. The name of his father and mother is not known.

[EDITOR'S NOTE: This editor researched a Urian Hosmer [sometimes also found as Uriah Osmore] of Onslow County, North Carolina {originally from Connecticut} who was enumerated on a 1769 and again on a 1770 early North Carolina Census along with three male Negros named London, Dover and Dick, and two female Negros named Dina and Sare. However, no children have been found linking him to the Osmore families of Greensville, Dinwiddie or Brunswick Counties, Virginia.]

[EDITOR'S NOTE: A second possibility for this (Unknown) Osmore is a James Osmer of Anson County [formed in 1749 from Bladen County], North Carolina who was enumerated on a 1763 early North Carolina Census. As an adult property owner in 1762, he would probably have been born in the 1730s or the very early 1740s. All other court house records were burned during the United States Civil War. To date, no evidence has been found linking him to the Osmore families of Greensville, Dinwiddie and/or Brunswick Counties, Virginia. According to a well-respected local genealogist, since most of the records of that era for Anson and Bladen Counties were destroyed, nothing else has been found for the name Osmer or the various other spellings associated with this surname.]

[EDITOR'S NOTE: A third, but slim, possibility for this (Unknown) Osmore is a Sylvester Hosmer, M.D. of Edenton, Chowan County, North Carolina who married Margaret (Unknown). Sylvester was born in 1765 and died 1794 in Chowan County and was buried there in the Johnston Cemetery. However, the only known son was James Johnson Hosmer, born in December 1791 and who died, age 19, in July 1811 at Edenton, Chowan County, North Carolina]

The Children of
(Unknown) Osmore

1. William Ozmore

probably born circa 1750/1755, probably in
Dinwiddie County, Virginia. His date and place of
death is not known. He married an unknown wife.
Her date and place of birth and death is not
known. The name of her father and mother is not
known. William and his unknown wife had at
least two children: Richard and William.

2. John W. Ozmore

born circa 1760/1765 in Dinwiddie County, Vir-
ginia. His date of death in Dinwiddie County,
Virginia is not known. He married Fannie (Un-
known). The date of their marriage, presumably in
Dinwiddie County, Virginia is not known. Her
date and place of birth and death is not known.
The name of her father and mother is not known.
He appears on the 1800 Virginia Tax List Index as
residing in Dinwiddie County, Virginia. John and
Fannie had at least two children:

a. Sarah Elizabeth Ozmore

born circa 1798 in Dinwiddie County, Virginia.
Her date and place of death is not known. She
married John C. Estes on December 30, 1819 in
Davidson County, Tennessee. He was born in

1794 in Virginia. He died in August 1863 in Davidson County, Tennessee. The name of his father and mother is not known. Sarah and John had at least four children: Theodoria Margaret, John Thomas, William Carroll and James [and there may have been two other daughters: Martha and Mary]. All the children were born in Tennessee.

b. Richard Ozmore
born circa 1799 in Dinwiddie County, Virginia. He died of consumption on June 9, 1874 in Brunswick County, Virginia. He married Nancy [also found as Sally on her daughter Martha's death record] (Unknown) sometime before 1828 [when their first child was born], presumably in Dinwiddie County, Virginia [it is known that he had relocated to the northern district of Brunswick County by June 1940, where he appears there on the U. S. Census, age 52, a shoemaker]. She was born in 1800 in Virginia. She died in 1866 in St. Andrews Parish, Brunswick County, Virginia. The name of her father and mother is not known.

Richard [then age 72] married, second, Elizabeth "Bettie" Newell [her surname from a previous marriage] on June 5, 1870 in Totaro, Brunswick County, Virginia. Elizabeth was born circa 1820 in Charlotte County, Virginia [in 1850, age 30, she was living in Prince George County, Virginia and in 1860 in the city of Petersburg, Dinwiddie County, Virginia]. Richard and Elizabeth had no issue.

Elizabeth [nee name unknown] had married, first, Ro(bert) M. Newell. He was born circa 1822 in Charlotte County, Virginia.

Richard Ozmar and his wife, Nancy appear in the Dinwiddie County, Virginia deed book [6, page 504] selling property to Paschal Tucker on October 20, 1850. It reads as follows:

This deed made this 20th day of October in the year 1850, between Richard Ozmar and Nancy his wife of the County of Brunswick of the one part, and Paschal Tucker of the County of Dinwiddie of the other part, whenceforth: that in consideration of the sum of eleven dollars to them in hand paid (the receipt whereof is hereby acknowledged to the said Richard Ozmar and Nancy his wife to grant unto the said Paschal Tucker all their right, title and interest in the lands of which (Jefe) Lewis dec'd ... died seized and possessed being nine and a half acres, by recent survey lying in the county of Dinwiddie and bounded by the lands of

Robert Minitree and said Paschal Tucker — to have and to hold the aforesaid rights, title and interest in and to the aforesaid piece or parcel of land and to and for his only proper use and behalf, free from the claim or claims of themselves, their heirs and assigns.

Witness our hands and seals the date above written:

Richard Ozmar (Seal)
Nancy Ozmar (Seal)

Richard's will [Brunswick County, Virginia Will Book 20, Page 271] reads as follows:

In the name of God Amen, I Richard Ozmar of the County of Brunswick, being sick and weak in body, but of sound mind and disposing memory and calling to mind the uncertainty of human life and being desirous to dispose of all such worldy estate as it hath pleasure God to bless me with, I give and bequeath the same in manner following, that is to say:

1st I desire all my just debts to be paid.

2nd I give and bequeath unto my wife Elizabeth Ozmar the following property to wit my cow,

Bett, my chamber bed, the prep and tableware therein, the dinner table, bureau, ½ dozen chairs and cooking utensils.

3rd I give and bequeath unto my daughter Indianna C. Ozmar my other bed, the second table and dressing table, the spinning wheel and two chairs.

4th I give and bequeath unto my three sons, J. R., H. B. and E.A. Ozmar all my shoe makers and farming tools to be equally divided among them.

5th I desire my other cow Blophum to be sold and the proceeds applied to my just debts and the remainder, if any, of said proceeds to be given to my grand daughter, Mary E. Ozmar.

6th I do hereby constitute and support my wife Elizabeth Ozmar Executrix of this my last will and testament hereby revoking all this or former wills or testaments by me heretofore made.

In witness hereof I have hereunto annexed my name and affix my seal this 20th day of February 1874.

Signed sealed & declared:

Richard Ozmore {Seal}

by Richd Ozmar as and for his last will & testament in the presence therein of us who at his request & in his presence have subscribed our names as witnesses.

Charles R. Short
Jno L. Short
Wm J. Cheely

Richard's will was later proved in Brunswick County Court during the August Term of 1874 as follows:

This last will and testament of Richard Osmore deceased was proved by the oaths of Charles R. Short & Wm. J. Cheely witnesses there to and ordered to be recorded and on the motion of Thomas J. Duane {the executrix therein named refusing to qualify} who made oath thereto according to law, and together with D. W. Spencer, C. R. Short and G. R. Mallary his securities entered into a bond in the penalty of $30.00 conditioned as the law directs, which bond was acknowledged by the several obligors therein named and ordered to be recorded.

Certificate is granted him for obtaining letters of Administration and the will (anneried) on the estate of said Richard Ozmore decd in due for,

Testa

E. R. Turnbill, Clerk

Richard and Nancy had six children:

1. Martha A. F. Ozmore
   born circa 1826 in Brunswick County, Virginia. She died, age 32, in July 1857 in Greensville County, Virginia. She married Albert Henry Martin on January 17, 1855 in Brunswick County, Virginia. He was born in 1825 in Brunswick County, Virginia. His date and place of death is not known. His father was Henry Martin of Brunswick County, Virginia. His mother was Ann (Unknown). Issue, if any, is not known.

2. John R. Ozmore
   born in 1829 in Brunswick County, Virginia. His date and place of death is not known. He married Susanna A. [another record says Susanna E.] Lunsford on December 25, 1850 in Brunswick County, Virginia. She was born

circa 1826 in Dinwiddie County, Virginia. She died, age 56, on June 4, 1882 in Chesterfield County, Virginia. Her father was William Lunsford of Dinwiddie County, Virginia. Her mother was Susan (Unknown) of Dinwiddie County, Virginia. John and Susanna had four children: Susan Amonelia "Anna," Algernon W. , John E. and James R. Edward.

3. William J. Ozmore

born in 1831 in Brunswick County, Virginia. His date and place of death is not known. He married Martha F.[7] Lanier on December 19, 1856 in Brunswick County, Virginia. She was born in 1836 in Brunswick County, Virginia. Her date and place of death is not known. Her father was Samuel[6] [David[5], William[4] {of Surry County, Virginia}, Thomas[3], Sampson[2] {of Charles City County, Virginia}, John[1] {of England}, John[1a] {of Lewisham, England}, Clement[2a] {of London, England}, Nicholas[3a] {of Rouen, France}, John[4a], Nicholas[5a] {born circa 1460}] Lanier of Brunswick County, Virginia. Her mother was Martha Saunders of Brunswick County, Virginia. Issue, if any, is not known.

4. Hartwell R. [aka Hartwell B.] Ozmore
born on July 5, 1834 in Brunswick County, Virginia. He died, age 69, in 1903 in Sturgeon, Brunswick County, Virginia. He married Parthenia King in 1859 in Brunswick County, Virginia. Her date and place of birth and death is not known. The name of her father is not known. Her mother was Elizabeth P. (Unknown) of Meherrin, Brunswick County, Virginia.

Hartwell enlisted in the Confederate Army on June 1861 at Norfolk, Virginia. He served two years in Company F, 12th Virginia Infantry Regiment. In his pension application, he stated that he was taken prisoner at Petersburg and was in prison when the war ended.

Hartwell and Parthenia had seven children: Lucy, James Benjamin Barham Beauregard, William Edward, Virginia [who died in infancy], Rosa A., Sarah P. and Charles Jefferson [all then known as Ozmar].

5. Edward A. Ozmore
born in 1836 in Dinwiddie County, Virginia. He died in 1912 in Nottaway County, Virginia. He married Sarah Jane Lucy on

December 17, 1867 at Totaro, Brunswick County, Virginia. She was born in 1840 in Brunswick County, Virginia. She died, age 31, on July 30, 1871 in Brunswick County, Virginia. Her father was John Jones [Jesse] Lucy of Brunswick County, Virginia. Her mother was Margaret B. Moore of Brunswick County, Virginia. Apparently, there was no issue.

Edward married, second, Margaret N. Lucy [Sarah Jane's sister] sometime before 1873 [when their first child was born] at either Totaro, Brunswick County or Sapony, Dinwiddie County, Virginia [where they were living in 1880]. She was born circa 1847 in Virginia. Her date and place of death is not known. Her father was John James [Jesse] Lucy of Brunswick County, Virginia. Her mother was Margaret B. Moore of Brunswick County, Virginia. Edward and Margaret had two children: John William and Robert L.

Edward served in the Confederate Army with Allen's Artillery. He enlisted on January 25, 1862 at St. John's Church in Lunenburg County, Virginia and served on the James River below Richmond during most of the war. On a retreat he was captured at Burkeville on April 6, 1865 and held at Point Lookout Prison until June 15, 1865.

6. Indianna C. "India" Ozmore
born circa 1838/1842 in Brunswick County, Virginia. Her date and place of death is not known. She married Gedie Jones [a widower] on January 10, 1852 in Dinwiddie County, Virginia. He was born circa 1830 in Dinwiddie County, Virginia. His date and place of death is not known. His father was Cary Jones of Dinwiddie County, Virginia. His mother was Elizabeth (Unknown) of Dinwiddie County, Virginia.

The Devader Family

The Life and Times of
Anna Emma[2] Devader

PATERNAL ANCESTRY: [DEVADER/
DUIVETTER: Peter Edward[1], Jacobus-Francies[1a]]

MATERNAL ANCESTRY: [COUSMAN/
COUSEMENT: Prudanse Sophie[1], Joseph E.[1a]]

ANNA EMMA[2] was born on December 21, 1898 at Morris, Wyandotte County, Kansas. She died on May 13, 1983 at the residence of her daughter, Bernadine Marie Higgins [nee Ozmer] at Annandale, Fairfax County, Virginia and was returned for burial in the Mount Calvary Cemetery at Topeka, Shawnee County, Kansas after services were held there at the Most Pure Heart of Mary Catholic

Anna Emma[2] Devader

Church. Her father was Peter Edward[1] Duivetter of Watervliet, Oost-Vlaanderen, Flanders, Belgium and later of Atkinson, Henry County, Illinois. Her mother was Prudanse Sophie[1] Cousman of St. Lauriens, Belgium and later of Atkinson, Henry County, Illinois.

135

Anna Emma[2] Devader
and Charles Henry[3]
Trezise

ANNA EMMA[2] married, first, Charles Henry[3] "Charley" Trezise on November 30, 1917 at Topeka, Shawnee County, Kansas by Ralph H. Gow, Probate Judge. Charles[3] was born on May 24 [another source says the 26th], 1893 [a twin], near Emmett, Pottawatomie County, Kansas. [Note: His twin brother, John[3], died when Charles[3] was a child]. Charles[3] died at age 25 years, 4 months, 22 days of influenza [during the pandemic of the Spanish Flu] on October 18, 1918 at Mecilla Park [University Park], Dona Aña County, New Mexico [other researchers say he died at the Army Barracks at State College, Arizona, but this is incorrect] and was returned home for burial. His father was Henry P.[2] [Henry P.[1] {of St. Just, Cornwall, England}, Henry[1a], Henry[2a]] Trezise of England, later of Michigan, and finally of Pottawatomie County, Kansas. His mother was Margaret Ellen [John {of Ohio and later of Adrian, Jackson County, Kansas}] Songs [his father's fourth wife] of Missouri City, Fort Bend County, Texas, and later of Jackson County, Kansas.

Charles[3] was a mechanic and taxi cab driver. In June 1917 he tried to enlist in the Army, but was turned down because of heart trouble. The next year he was drafted. When he told them about his heart condition, they told him there was no record and accused him of trying to get out of his military obligation because he had just married and started a family. At the time of his death he was an instructor of truck driving for the U. S. Army. His funeral services were conducted by Reverend Ellington. Music was furnished by a chorus of friends. The Masons conducted funeral services under the direction of Oscar Strain, followed by full military honors. A firing squad from Topeka attended the funeral under the command of Captain Erwin and Lieutenant Heidt. While the beautiful song *Keep the Home Fires Burning* was being sung, the body was laid to rest in the family lot at the Adrian Cemetery in Jackson County, Kansas.

Anna Devader
& Jack Ozmer

ANNA EMMA[2] married, second, Windsor Wilkerson "Jack" Ozmer of Fairburn, Fulton County, Georgia and later of St. Marys Pottawa-, tomie County, Kansas on February 8, 1921 at Kinney Heights [a district of Kansas

City], Wyandotte County, Kansas. The ceremony was performed in the Sacred Hearts Catholic Church by William DeBoeck, Rector. "Jack" was born on September 26, 1882 at Fairburn, Fulton County, Georgia. He died of acute coronary occlusion [heart attack] at 3:00 am on June 16, 1963 at Ault's Nursing Home at St. Marys, Pottawatomie County, Kansas and was buried there in the Mount Calvary Cemetery. His father was Jefferson Gadwell [Robert Clark, Richard, (William)] Ozmer of DeKalb County and later of Fairburn, Fulton County, Georgia. His mother was Ella Jane Hunter of Georgia.

ANNA EMMA[2] was the sixth of seven children. While a child, as "payment" for a week's work, her father would let her "look at" a brand new shiny dime, while her brothers were paid 50 cents. Sometimes her mother would sneak her 3 cents for candy. There is a story about her father having a friend named Van Rogen, who went by the nickname "White Head," since his hair was so white. When Anna was seven, "White Head" asked her to show him where her dad kept his beer. She showed him. "I sure got punished for that," Anna said. After she was married, she took in wash and worked as an aide in "confinement cases" for $1.25 per day [24 hours shifts]. Confinement cases were new mothers who were bed-ridden from the birth of a child until two weeks after.

ANNA EMMA[2]'s children were all born at home. The family story is, when her husband-to-be, "Jack," told his sister that he was going to marry Anna, the sister wrote to and warned Anna not to marry him, as he was a drunkard and a wanderer. When "Jack" still lived in Georgia with his parents, he was known to say he was going out for cigarettes, then not return for months. Oddly enough, "Jack" knew Anna's first husband Charles[3] Trezise, who was a mechanic and drove an old Ford as a taxi cab operator. They both worked in the same garage, where "Jack" had trained him as a mechanic. When Charles[3] went into the military, he had asked "Jack" to look after his wife.

ANNA EMMA[2] related that while married to "Jack," she paid all the bills since, according to her, "Jack" was irresponsible and would spend all their money on booze. Anna[2] claimed he was known as the town drunk; however, their daughters believe that their mother only said that because she was bitter about their failed marriage; that, in fact, there was a town drunk and his name was "Bat Eye" Higgins. Also, according to Anna[2], the first years of their marriage they lived off the $10,000 proceeds of Anna's insurance money, received after the death of her first husband. Anna claimed that Jack had known about the insurance policy before Charlie[3] Trezise died and that he'd married her just to get at the money. One day, at breakfast, when their daughter, "Peg," turned

16 [in 1938], Anna[2] gave "Jack" an ultimatum: "Pay the bills and be a better husband and father, or don't show up here tonight." His reply was, "Nobody works me to death." He didn't come home that night. In 1952, Anna[2] lived at 907 Green Street, Topeka, Shawnee County, Kansas, where she worked for many years with the Singer Sewing Machine Corporation Later, after her children were married and left home, she was employed as a nanny with a family in Texas. Ultimately, she moved in with her daughter, Bernadine Marie, at Fairfax, Fairfax County, Virginia and later at Annandale, Fairfax County, Virginia where, in 1983, she died.

Tombstone of
Anna Emma Devader Ozmer

The Children of
Anna Emma[2] Devader
and Charles Henry[3] Trezise

1. Charles Henry[4] Trezise
born on August 27, 1918 at Emmett, Pottawatomie County, Kansas. He died an infant of leakage of the heart on October 10, 1918 at Emmet, Pottawatomie County, Kansas and was buried there next to his father.

The Children of
Anna Emma[2] Devader
and Windsor Wilkerson "Jack" Ozmer

(T-L to R) Robert & Marie Higgins, Anna Devader Ozmer, "Peg" Allen & Bernard Ozmer (B-L to R) Donna Higgins and Linda Allen

2. Margaret Ella Leotha "Peg" Ozmer
born on October 4, 1922 at St. Marys, Pottawatomie County, Kansas. She married Roy William[2] Allen on February 23, 1946 in the Assumption Catholic Church at Topeka, Shawnee County, Kansas. Roy[2] was born on May 1, 1921 at St. Marys, Pottawatomie County, Kansas. He died on October 2, 2002 at Topeka, Shawnee County, Kansas and was buried there in Mount Calvary Cemetery. His father was Ernest Gotfried[1] [Turie E.[1a] {afa Trure E.}] Allen of Vadstena, Gotland, Sweden [Editor's Note: Vadstena is a small town noted for its lace. It is located on the island of Gotland on the east coast of Sweden, south of Stockholm]. His mother was Mary Martha [Henry] Eichman [Ernest[1]'s second wife] of Flush, Pottawatomie County, Kansas. Margaret currently [2015] resides at Topeka, Shawnee County, Kansas. Margaret and Roy[2] had three children: Linda Marie[3], Patricia Ann[3] and Robert William[3].

3. Bernadine Marie Prudence "Pud" Ozmer
born on November 4, 1925 at St. Marys, Pottawatomie County, Kansas. She married Robert Charles[4] Higgins on July 23, 1945 at Washington, D.C. Robert[4] was born on March 16, 1925 at Washington, D.C. He died of lung cancer on February 19, 1982 at home at Fairfax, Fairfax County, Virginia. His father was Joseph Francis[3]

[John Joseph[2], John[1] {of Ireland}] Higgins of Schenectady, Schenectady County, New York and later of Washington, D.C. and Alexandria, Virginia. His mother was Margaret Ellen [William Henry, Alvah, William, Joseph, Joseph {of Massachusetts}] Pitts of Castleton, Rensselaer County, New York. Bernadine currently [2015] resides at Port St. Lucie, St. Lucie County, Florida. Bernadine and Robert[4] had three children: Donna Marie[5], Karen Ellen[5] [a twin] and Sharon Ann[5] [a twin].

4. LeRoy Robert Ozmer
born on December 5, 1928 at St. Marys, Pottawatomie County, Kansas. He died an infant of chicken pox on November 17, 1929 at St. Marys, Pottawatomie County, Kansas.

5. Bernard Francis James Ozmer
born on November 30, 1931 at St. Marys, Pottawatomie County, Kansas. He died of lung cancer at 3:00 pm on December 17, 1986 at his home at Emmett, Gem County, Idaho. He married, first, Jeanetta Irene[3] "Jean" Durault on May 30, 1956 at Tucson, Pima County, Arizona. They were later divorced in April 1976 in Contra Costa County, California. Jeanetta[3] was born on January 14, 1938 at Westford, Middlesex County, Massachusetts. Her father was Armand R.[2] [Aime[1] {afa Eurie Durot of Tingwick, Athabasca, Quebec Province,

Canada and later of Lowell, Middlesex County, Massachusetts}, Emelie -Onezine[1a] {afa Onesime of Puisieulx, France}] Dureault of Lowell, Middlesex County, Massachusetts and later of Tucson, Pima County, Arizona. Her mother was Irene Alice[2] [Joseph Etienne[1] {of Nicolet, Quebec Province, Canada}, Adolphe[1a], Jean B.[2a], Louis F.[3a], Augustin[4a] {of Quebec, Quebec Province, Canada}, Louis[5a] {Parmentier Lyonnais {of Lyon, Rhone, Rhone-Alpes, France}] Parmentier of Lowell, Middlesex County, Massachusetts and later of Tucson, Pima County, Arizona. Bernard and Jeanetta[3] had five children: Bernard Francis, Jr., Michael Lee, Steven Christopher, David William and Debra Ann.

Jeannette[2] "Jean" married, second, Scott Carson[11] Wells on September 30, 1982 at Watford, Herfordshire, England. Scott[11] was born on February 11, 1940 at Los Angeles, Los Angeles County, California. His father was Scott Carson[10] [Ebenezer[9] {afa Ebenezer of South Carolina}, Eliza Sewell[8] Wells {who had Ebenezer by Henry Lawrence Britton of South Carolina, who died in the U. S. Civil War during the Battle of Manassas}, Ebenezer[7] {of Warren, Knox County, Maine}, Ebenezer[6], Robert[5], Nathaniel[4] {of Newbury, Essex County, Massachusetts}, Thomas[3], John[2] {of Ipswich, Essex County, Massachusetts}, Thomas[1] {of Essex County, England}, Thomas[1a] {of Essex, Lancaster, England}, Thomas[2a]] Wells, Sr. of California. His mother was Lila Mary [Ponciano J. "Ponce" of Idaho}] Jimenez of Sacramento, Sacramento County, California. Jean[2] and Scott[11] had no issue.

Bernard married, second, Geraldine Rae[6] "Gerrie" Clure on March 16, 1979 and the marriage was recorded on March 19, 1979 at Reno, Washoe County, Nevada. Geraldine[6] was born on November 21, 1950 in St. Patrick's Hospital at Missoula, Missoula County, Montana [Editor's Note: The family actually lived at Stephen's Mountain]. Her father was Kenneth Miller[5] [Asher Enos[4] {of Crawford, Dawes County, Nebraska}, John Baptiste[3] {of Naperville, Dupage County, Illinois}, Joseph[2] {of Canada and later of Iowa}, John[1] {born circa 1790/1795 of Switzerland and later of Canada and finally of Minnesota, where he died in 1862}] Clure of Laramie County, Wyoming. Her mother was Ruby Patricia[3] [Jonas A.[2] {afa Joseph of Verona, Lawrence County, Missouri}, William[1] {of England and later of Missouri}] Garrod of Hamilton, Ravelli County, Montana. Bernard and Geraldine[6] had no issue.

Geraldine[6] married, first, Russell Clifford Terry. They later divorced. His father was Hillard H. Terry of Colorado. His mother was Maxine (Unknown) of Colorado. Geraldine[6] and Russell had a child: Ginger Rae Terry.

Geraldine[6] married, second, Wallace Edgar Martin on March 15, 1972 in Humboldt County, Oklahoma. The marriage was recorded there on March 23, 1972. They later divorced. His adoptive father was William Martin of Alabama. His mother was Dolly (Unknown). There was no issue.

Geraldine[6] married, fourth, Danny Leo Green on November 28, 1987 [recorded on December 2, 1987] in Clark County, Nevada. They later divorced. His father was Thomas Leo Green of Ada County, Idaho. His mother was Harriet May Lake of Ada County, Idaho. There was no issue.

Geraldine[6] married, fifth, Bernard Vincent Montgomery on October 4, 1994 in Yamhill County, Oregon. They later divorced. There was no issue.

The Family of Peter Edward & Prudanse D'huyvettere
(L to R; B to T) Anna Emma, Henry; Peter, Prudanse, John;
Charlie, Edward, Mary and Alfred

The Life and Times of
Peter Edward[1] D'huyvettere
[Also found as Duivetter and Devetter]

PATERNAL ANCESTRY: [DEVETTER/ DUIVETTER/D'HUYVETTERE: Jacobus-Francies[1a]]

MATERNAL ANCESTRY: [DE SMET: Joesphine/Seraphina[1], Jacob Bernardus[1a]]

PETER EDWARD[1] was born on February 22, 1860 a Water-vliet, Flanders, Oost-Vlaander-en, Belgium [Editor's Note: Watervliet is a quiet rural town in the Meetjesland in the Flanders area of Belgium on the border with Zeeland, which is now part of The Netherlands. Watervliet was named after a family of the same name.]. He died on March 16, 1929 at Emmet,

Peter Edward D'huyvettere

Pottawatomie County, Kansas and was buried there in the Holy Cross Cemetery. His father was Jacob-Francies[1a] D'Huyvettere of Flanders, Belgium. His mother was Josephine/Seraphina[1a] DeSmet [May 10, 1832-1914 and buried in a convent at Basseville, Belgium] of Watervliet, Flanders, Belgium, daughter of Jacob Berndardus[2a] DeSmet and Sophie[2a] Heetezone of Watervliet, Oost-Vlaanderen, Flanders, Belgium.

Peter & Prudanse Devader

PETER EDWARD[1] married, first, Prudanse Sophie[1] Cousman [afa Coesman and Cousement] on October 19, 1885, after the marriage license was granted on October 3, 1885. They were married in St. Anthony's Catholic Church at Atkinson, Henry County, Illinois. She was born on June 7, 1863 at St. Lauriens, East Flanders, Belgium. She died on June 28, 1914 at Emmet, Pottawatomie, Kansas and was buried there in the Holy Cross Cemetery. Her father was Joseph E.[1a] "Leo" Cousman [also found as Cousement] of St. Lauriens, Flanders, Belgium. Her mother was Marie Therese[1a] [Anthony[2a]] DeVos of St. Lauriens, Flanders, Belgium. The family story is that Prudanse[1] came over to join her sister Louise[1] Vandervelde of Holy Cross, Kansas. They came on the same ship with the D'Huyvetteres, where she met Peter[1], whom she later married in Illinois.

Joseph[1a] Cousman and his wife Marie[1a] ground grain into flour as a living while they lived in Belgium. During an electrical storm with high winds, Joseph[1a] was caught in the grist mill wheel, ruptured his

150

spleen and bled to death. His daughter, Prudanse Sophie[1], was one of four children. The others were Louise Marie[1] [who married August Charles[1] Vandevalde of Mule Viche, Belgium], Vildi and a son who died at age eleven.

After Joseph[1a]'s death, his wife Marie[1a] married Peter J.[1a] "Sa Sa" DeWendt on April 29, 1868 in Pottawatomie County, Kansas. He was born on March 7, 1835 at St. Lauriens, East Flanders, Belgium. His date and place of death is not known. His father was Jean Baptiste[2a] DeWendt of St. Lauriens, East Flanders, Belgium. His mother was Joanne[2a] Claeys of St. Lauriens, East Flanders, Belgium. Peter[1a] DeWendt owned a tavern in Belgium. Peter[1a] and Marie[1a] had two sons: Henry[1] and Jules[1]. When Peter[1a] was alive, they lived in the nearby town and walked three miles every day to their farms. They'd take their cattle to pasture and stop at the DeWendt tavern for beer, which is how Peter[1a] and Marie[1a] knew each other. After Peter[1a] died, Marie[1a] brought the two DeWendt sons and joined her other children in Illinois.

PETER EDWARD[1] married, second, Justine DeWilde-DeCuyper in 1919 in Kansas. They were separated in 1925. According to family gossip, she took him for all he had. She was born on May 3, 1863 at Watervliet, Flanders, Belgium. Apparently, at some point, she returned to Belgium, because researchers indicate that she died on March 13, 1960 at Watervliet, Oost-Vlaanderen, Flanders Belgium. The name of her father and mother is not known. There was no issue from this marriage.

PETER EDWARD[1]'s second wife's father, Jacob Bernardus[1a] DeSmet, and his wife, Sophie[1a] Heetezone, had two other children besides Seraphine, namely, Edvard[1] and Pieter[1], both of Watervliet, Oost-Vlaanderen, Belgium.

PETER EDWARD[1] and Prudanse Sophie[1] Cousman both left Belgium by ship, where they met, then landed in New York City after a two week sailing voyage. He settled, temporarily, in Pittsburg, Pennsylvania before traveling on to Illinois circa 1884, where they were married in 1885. They then moved on to Kansas, where they settled for the rest of their life.

PETER EDWARD[1] and Prudanse Sophie[1] presumably moved to Shawnee Mission Township, Kansas soon after they married, as several of their children were born there. Apparently, they later moved to Morris, Wyandotte County, Kansas where at least their last two children were born. On the 1895 U. S. Census for the State of Kansas, the spelling of the D'Huyvetter/Duivetter name was Duvatter. They lived with their family of seven children in the Shawnee Mission

Township and owned 100 acres of land, 66 of which were under cultivation. Sometime after that, they moved to the city of Adrian, Jackson County, Kansas, near Little Cross Creek, which was approximately four miles from Holy Cross. After the railroad going west came through and bypassed both communities, the town of Emmett was formed and Adrian and Holy Cross were abandoned. It was sometime after 1895 that the family name was changed to Devader, which is its present day spelling. The original surname seems to be taken from the sign of the cross, and is believed to be associated with "En dem nom de vader," meaning "In the name of the father."

PETER EDWARD[1] owned a section of land in Morris, Wyandotte County, Kansas amounting to one square mile [one of the 36 subdivisions of the township] where he grew corn, wheat, oats, potatoes and alfalfa. He also raised cows, pigs, horses and chickens. He did the farming and the children bundled the produce. He would take the children to market every other day. He took the large potatoes to market, ate the medium ones, and the small ones he boiled and fed to the pigs. On a successful day he would return home, down the long lane to his house, singing in Flemish, "Viva, viva." When he arrived with his money, he put it in a coffee can.

PETER EDWARD[1] was remembered as being a stocky built man with a red mustache [his mother had red hair], who drank beer and wine, smoked cigars and breathed very heavy. He used to make homemade wine and put it in fruit jars and bottles, then bury them, he was forever forgetting where. He also didn't trust the banks and buried his money in tobacco tins. It is said that his son Charles[2] once had a dream, remembering seeing where his father had buried one of his treasured bottles of wine. When he woke up, he went out behind a shed and, to his surprise, there it was.

PETER EDWARD[1] was, according to his passport dated April 1927 [two years before his death], 5' 6" tall with gray hair and brown eyes. That year, he made a trip to Belgium to visit with his relatives who had remained there.

The Children of
Peter Edward[1] D'huyvettere
[Also found as Duivetter and Devetter]
and Prudanse Sophie[1] Cousman

1. Mary Josephine[2] "Louise" Devetter/Devader
   born on August 22, 1886 in Shawnee County,
   Kansas. She died, age 23 years, 2 months, 27 days,
   on November 19, 1909 [two days after the birth of
   her second child, Mary Josephine[4]] at Emmet,
   Pottawatomie County, Kansas and was buried
   there in the Holy Cross Cemetery. She married
   John Bernard[3] DeLeye of Shawnee County, Kansas
   on November 5, 1907 at Emmet, Pottawatomie
   County, Kansas by the Reverend Father Meehan at
   the chapel of the Emmet Parochial School, later to
   be known as the Holy Cross Church. They were
   the first couple married in that church. John[3] was
   born on April 10, 1882 in Shawnee County,
   Kansas. He died on April 10, 1961, presumably in
   Pottawatomie County, Kansas. His father was
   Charles[2] [Jacob[1] {of Belgium and later of Oregon}]
   DeLeye of Platte City, Platte County, Missouri. His
   mother was Anna "Annie" Frathauf of Shawnee
   County, Kansas. Mary Josephine[2] and John[3] had
   two children:

a. Anna Christine[4] "Annie" DeLeye
born on October 3, 1908 at Emmett, Pottawatomie County, Kansas and was the first child baptized there at the Holy Cross Church. She died on February 14, 2000 at Overland Park, Johnson County, Kansas. She married Henry Joseph[2] Soetaert on June 12, 1928 in the Holy Cross Church at Emmett, Pottawatomie County, Kansas. He was born on March 7, 1903 at Kansas City, Jackson County, Missouri. He died on February 14, 1986 at Overland Park, Johnson County, Kansas. His father was Louis Carel[1] [Petrus Charles[1a] {of Pittem, West-Vlaanderen, Belgium}, Amand[2a] {of Oostrozebeke, West-Vlaanderen, Belgium}, Jan Martin[3a], Joost[4a], Petrus[5a] {born 1696}] Soetaert of Egem, Belgium. His mother was Elizabeth Ann Huls of Dorchester, Allamakee County, Iowa. Anna[4] and Henry[2] had five children: Mary Louise[3], Barbara Ann[3], Leonard Joseph[3], Bernard Louis[3] and Michael Anthony[3].

b. Mary Josephine[4] DeLeye
born on November 17, 1909 at Emmett, Pottawatomie County, Kansas. She died on April 12, 2008 at Fairfield, Solano County, California. She married Robert Wayne[4] Murray of Balko, Beaver County, Oklahoma on June 9, 1932 in Jackson County, Missouri. He was born on

August 16, 1906 at Balko, Beaver County, Oklahoma. He died on September 12, 1982 at Orangevale, Sacramento County, California. His father was Robert John[3] [Joseph R.[2], Jr. {of Aurora, Kane County, Illinois}, Joseph R.[1] {of Lower Canada}, Michael[1a] {Morin}] Murray of Joliet, Will County, Illinois. His mother was Ella Mae [Charles Asbury {of Fayette County, Oklahoma}, Eli {of Sussex County, Delaware}, Eli Henry {of Lexington, Fayette County, Kentucky}, Elijah "Eli" {of Worcester County, Maryland}, George {of Talbot County, Maryland}, Thomas {born 1675 Eastern Shore, Virginia}] West of Pringham, O'Brien County, Iowa. Mary[4] and Robert[4] had six children: Mary Etta[5], Delores Ann[5], Patricia Josephina[5], (child)[5], Timothy Wayne[5] and John Bernard[5].

[EDITOR'S NOTE: After their mother died in 1909, John[3] DeLeye, who worked for the railroad, wasn't able to be home to raise them. On the 1915 Kansas State Census, John[3] and his daughters Anna Christine[4], age 6, and Mary Josephine[4], age 5, were living with the family of C.J. and Hellen Martin and their son Oscar, along with a woman named Julia Brown, age 62. Then, on the 1920 U. S. Census, Anna[4], age 11, and Mary[4], age 10, were enumerated at the Sisters of Charity Catholic Orphanage known as St. Vincent's Home at

Delaware, Levenworth County, Kansas. However, on the 1925 Kansas State Census, they were back home living with their father.]

John[3] married, second, Mary Magdelena[3] "Lena" Ketter on August 5, 1929 in the Holy Cross Catholic Church at Emmett, Pottawatomie County, Kansas. Mary[3] was born on April 3, 1897 at St. Benedict, Nemaha County, Kansas. She died on January 5, 1979 at St. Marys, Pottawatomie County [another researcher says Topeka, Shawnee County], Kansas and was buried there in the Mt. Calvary Catholic Church Cemetery. Her father was Philipp[2] [Philipp[1] {of Zilshausen, Cochem-Zell, Rheinland-Pfalz, Deutschland/Germany}, Johann Joseph[1a], Antonio[2a], Johann Jakob[3a]] Ketter of St. Nazianz, Mantowoc County, Wisconsin. Her mother was Elizabeth Ann[2] [Henry[1] {of Hannover, Stadt Hannover, Niedesachsen, Germany}, Bernhard Meinrich[1a]] Huls of Dorchester, Allamakee County, Iowa. John[3] and Mary[3] had two children: Charles D.[4] and Margaret[4].

2. Edward Joseph[2] [afa Edw John] Devetter/Devader born on April 3, 1888 in Shawnee County, Kansas. He died on August 27, 1959, presumably in Kansas. He married Marie Natalie[2] DeWilde on August 13, 1913, presumably in Delia, Jackson County, Kansas, where she was residing at the

time. Marie[2] was born on September 11, 1894 at Botte Laere, Belgium. She died on January 7, 1992 at Scranton, Osage County, Kansas. Her father was (Unknown)[1] DeWilde of Botte Laere, Belgium. Her mother was Justine[1] (Unknown) of Botte, Laere, Belgium. Marie[2] came to the United States in 1911 on a ship named *The Kroonland*. She lived for one year in St. Marys, Pottawatomie County, Kansas before she moved to Delia, Jackson County, Kansas where she was married. Edward Joseph[2] and Marie[2] had ten children:

a. Anna Marie[3] Devader
born on December 21, 1916 at Emmett, Pottawatomie County, Kansas. She died on August 18, 2010 in the St. Mary's Manor at St. Marys, Pottawatomie County, Kansas. She married Ralph Wathel[11] Morford on September 2, 1935 in The Holy Cross Catholic Church at Emmett, Pottawatomie County, Kansas. He was born on February 5, 1913 at Soldier, Jackson County, Kansas. He died on January 18, 1989 at Onaga, Pottawatomie County, Kansas and was buried in the Holy Cross Catholic Church Cemetery at Emmett. His father was Ross William[10] [William Isaac[9] {of Madison County, Ohio}, Isaac Newton[8] {of Wooster, Wayne County, Ohio}, Abraham[7] {of Newcastle, Newcastle County, Delaware}, Frederick[6], Isaac[5] {of Cumberland

County, New Jersey}, Cornelius[4] {of Burlington County, New Jersey}, John[3] {of Cranberry, Middlesex County, New Jersey}, Thomas[2] {of Middletown, Monmouth County, New Jersey}, John[1] {of England}, John[1a] {Morfit of Bath, Easton, England}, Thomas[2a], Richard[3a]] Morford of Reilly, Nemaha County, Kansas. His mother was Margaret E. Suter of Kansas. Anna[3] and Ralph[11] had four children: Joanne[12], Jeannie[12], Don[12] and Holton[12].

b. Edward H.[3] Devader
born on July 30, 1918 at Emmett, Pottawatomie County, Kansas. He died on April 11, 2010 at the home of his daughter, Barbara[4], at St. Marys, Pottawatomie County, Kansas and was buried in the Holy Cross Catholic Church at Emmett. He married Pauline Henrietta Lysek. She was born on February 2, 1919 at Washington, Jackson County, Kansas. She died on May 22, 1989 at Delia, Jackson County, Kansas. Her father was Louis Henry Lysek of Washington, Jackson County, Kansas. Her mother was Mary Theresa[2] [Frank[1] {of Austria}, Jan[1a], Nicholas[2a], Valentine[3a]] Simecka of Delia, Jackson County, Kansas. Edward[3] and Pauline had nine children: Mary Lou[4], Barbara[4] "Bobbi," Karen[4], Mark[4] [who died stillborn], Linda[4], Donna[4], Gregory[4], Marvin[4] and Kevin[4].

Edward[3] married, second, Bonnie Marie Laswell on August 12, 1991 in Potawatomie County, Kansas. She was born on November 19, 1933 at rural Onaga, Potawatomie County, Kansas. She died, age 77, on November 12, 2010 at her home at Emmett, Potawatomie County, Kansas and was buried there in the St. Clair Cemetery. Her father was Fred G. [Harvey Anderson {of Leavenworth County, Kansas}] Lassswell of Pottawatomie County, Kansas. Her mother was Gwendolyn Marie [Steward {of Michgan}] Henderson of near Louisville, Pottawatomie County, Kansas. Edward[3] and Bonnie had no issue.

Bonnie had married, first, Raphael A. Meyer. They later divorced. Bonnie and Raphael had one child: Alan.

c. Helen Bernice[3] Devader
born on April 18, 1920 at Emmett, Pottawatomie County, Kansas. She died, age 87, on September 1, 2007 at Eugene, Land County, Oregon. She married Edward John[3] Helget on May 9, 1939 at St. Marys, Pottawatomie County, Kansas. He was born on June 9, 1914 in Pottawatomie County, Kansas. He died on May 3, 1996 at Junction City, Lane County, Oregon and later buried at Eugene. His father was Henry J.[2]

[George[1] {of Germany}] Helget of Kansas. His mother was Rose A.[2] [(Unknown)[1] {of Germany}] (Unknown) of Kansas. Helen[3] and Edward had two children: Rita[4] and Betty[4].

d. Raphael J.[3] "Ray"Devader
born on July 31, 1923 at Emmett, Pottawatomie County, Kansas. He died on December 25, 1994 at Emmett, Pottawatomie County, Kansas. Apparently, he went out on a drive on Christmas day, parked the car, went to sleep in the back seat and never woke up. He was buried there in the Holy Cross Catholic Church Cemetery. He had been in the St. Mary's Nursing Home since 1985.

e. Joseph Charles[3] Devader
born on December 22, 1924 at Emmett, Pottawatomie County, Kansas. He died on June 1, 2002 in a hospital at Onago, Pottawatomie County, Kansas. He married Catherine Louise[3] Martin on August 26, 1950 in the St. Stanislaus Church at Rossville, Shawnee County, Kansas. She was born on January 10, 1932 in Kansas. Her father was Henry Miller[2] [(Unknown)[1] {of Germany}] Marton of Maple Hill, Wabaunsee County, Kansas. Her mother was Edith Esabelle [Joseph {of Indiana}] Burns of Kansas. Joseph[3] and Catherine[3] had ten children: Lawrence

Eugene[4], Edith Marie[4], David Duane[4], Loretta[4], Marcia Joleen[4], Robert Ray[4] [a twin], Roberta Kay[4] [a twin], Gerald Joseph[4], Renae Louise[4] [a twin] and Ronald Louis[4] [a twin, who died after 27 days].

f. Henry Raymond[3] Devader
born on May 30, 1927 at Emmett, Pottawatomie County, Kansas. His date and place of death is not known. He married Elaine Ann Mulligan on October 13, 1956 in the Holy Cross Church at Emmett, Pottawatomie County, Kansas. She was born on May 29, 1935 at Emmett, Pottawatomie County, Kansas. Henry[3] and Elaine had four children: Steven Joseph[4], Michael James[4], Kathleen Ann[4] and Jeannette Louise[4].

g. Leonard[3] Devader
born on November 10, 1931 at Emmett, Pottawatomie County, Kansas. He married Geraldine[3] Vap on January 16, 1957 in the Sacred Heart Church at Atwood, Rawlins County, Kansas. They divorced in 1978. She was born on July 11, 1933 at Atwood, Rawlins County, Kansas. She died, age 76, on March 23, 2010 at Topeka, Shawnee County, Kansas. Her father was Joseph Fredereick[2] [Fred[1] {of Dolni, Loucky, Moravia and later of the Deweese area, Clay County, Nebraska}, Frantisek[1a] "Frank,"

Ignac[2a]] Vap of Rawlins County, Kansas. Her mother was Annastasia[2] "Anna" [John F.[1] {of Moravia}, Frank[1a]] Kacirek of Rawlins County, Kansas. Leonard[3] and Geraldine[3] had four children: Diana Lynn[4], Bruce DeWayne[4], Cynthia Suzanne[4] and Curt Douglas[4].

Geraldine[3] married, second, Clifton Marvin Lane sometime after 1978, presumably at Topeka, Shawnee County, Kansas. He was born on June 14, 1927 at Topeka, Shawnee County, Kansas. He died on January 21, 1981 at Topeka, Shawnee County, Kansas. His father was Shirley C. [Brook Claude, John William {of Tennessee}] Lane of Topeka, Shawnee County, Kansas. His mother was Mabel Irene[3] [William Tell[2], Sr., Jacob[1] {of Switzerland, who died in 1864 in a U.S. Civil War Confederate Prison at Huntsville, Texas}] Landis of Topeka, Shawnee County, Kansas.

h. Mary Kay[3] Devader
born on February 16, 1936 at Emmett, Pottawatomie County, Kansas. She died on August 6, 2012 in the Golden Living Center at Neodesha, Wilson County, Kansas and was buried in the Mount Hope Cemetery at Independence, Montgomery County, Kansas. She married John Mathew Berberick on August

20, 1955 at Emmett, Pottawatomie County, Kansas. He was born on June 12, 1936 at Topeka, Shawnee County, Kansas. He died on January 31, 1997 at Independence, Montgomery County, Kansas and was buried there in the Calvary Independence Cemetery. Mary Kay[3] and John had six children: Mark Eugene, Thomas Lee, Douglas Wayne, Johnna Kay, Elizabeth Marie and Patricia Ann.

i. Theresa Louise[3] Devader
born on July 4, 1937 at Emmett, Pottawatomie County, Kansas. She died an infant on January 30, 1939 at Emmett, Potawattomie County, Kansas.

j. Donald Dean[3] Devader
born on February 9, 1939 at Emmett, Pottawatomie County, Kansas. He married Judy Ann Ronnau on September 5, 1959, probably at Manhattan, Riley County, Kansas, where her parents lived at the time. She was born on October 24, 1941, probably in Pottawatomie County, Kansas. Her father was John C. Ronnau of St. Marys, Pottawatomie County, Kansas. Her mother was M. June [T. P. "Pete"] Melenson of St. Marys, Pottawatomie County, Kansas. Donald[3] and Judy had five children: Christy Lee[4], Tara Suzanne[4], Trent Andrew[4],

Scott Jeffrey[4] and Alison Marie[4].

3. John Thomas[2] Devetter/Devader
born on October 4, 1890 in Shawnee County,
Kansas. He died on July 12, 1973 at Lenexa,
Johnson County, Kanas and was buried there in
the St. John's Cemetery. He married Mary[1]
Brouckaert {Brouchaert} on April 23, 1923 in Kan-
sas. She was born on June 28, 1889 at Wyngne,
Belgium. She died on August 24, 1952 and was
buried in St. John's Cemetery at Lenexa, Johnson
County, Kansas. Her father was August[1a] Brouc-
haert of Wyngne, Belgium. Her mother was Julia[1a]
Rotty of Wyngne, Belgium. John Thomas[2] and
Mary[1] had four children:

a. Rose Mary[3] Devader
born on February 12, 1924 in Jackson County,
Kansas. She died on July 24, 1989 at Downey,
Hospital County, California and brought home
to be buried in St. John's Catholic Cemetery at
Lenexa, Johnson County, Kansas. She married
Carl Eugene Wey on March 1, 1946 at Kansas
City, Kansas. They were later divorced. He was
born on July 13, 1922 at Lenexa, Johnson
County, Kansas. He died on March 11, 1988 in
Johnson County, Kansas [another record says
Cobb County, Georgia]. The name of his father
and mother is not known. He enlisted in the U.

S. Army during Word War II on May 12, 1941 at Fort Leavenworth, Kansas as a Private in the Infantry. Rose[3] and Carl had four children: Robert Lewis "Bob," Roberta Jean, James Michael and Dianne Marie "Diana."

b. Elizabeth Ann[3] Devader [a twin]
born on January 20, 1927 in Jackson County, Kansas. Her date and place of death is not known. She married Walter Jack Begley II in April 1966. Elizabeth[3] and Walter had one child: Walter Jack III.

c. Mary Louise[3] Devader [a twin]
born on January 20, 1927 in Jackson County, Kansas. She died at birth.

d. John Joseph[3] Devader
born on May 25, 1932 in Jackson County, Kansas. He died at birth.

4. Charles Edward[2] Devetter/Devader
born on June 30, 1892 in Shawnee County, Kansas. He died on March 15, 1969 at Emmett, Pottawatomie County, Kansas and was buried there in the Holy Cross Cemetery. He married Margaret Virginia[2] [also shown in some files as Margaret Ann] "Maggie" Glick on April 22, 1919, presumably in Pottawatomie County, Kansas. She was

born on December 28, 1897 at St. Marys, Pottawatomie County, Kansas. She died on November 16, 1966 in her home at Emmett, Pottawatomie, Kansas and was buried there in the Holy Cross Cemetery. Her father was John Peter[1] [Nicholas Seitz[1a], Peter[2a], Karl[3a] {of Koehler, Russia}, Frantz Joseph[4a] {of Wertheim, Germany}] Glick of Mariental, Russia. Her mother was Mary Dora[1] [Nicholas[1a]] Buchholz of Graf, Russia. Charles E.[2] and Margaret[2] had eight children:

a. (son)[3] Devader
   stillborn on April 4, 1920 at Emmett, Pottawatomie County, Kansas.

b. Charles Aloysious[3] Devader
   born on February 14, 1921 at Emmett, Pottawatomie County, Kansas. He died on September 14, 1995 at Emmett, Pottawatomie County, Kansas and was buried there in the Holy Cross Cemetery. He married Mae Edith[4] Kovar on October 23, 1943 at Emmett, Pottawatomie County, Kansas. She was born on January 29, 1925 at Rossville, Shawnee County, Kansas. She died on June 26, 1996 at St. Marys, Pottawatomie County, Kansas and was buried there at the Holy Cross Cemetery. Her father was Edward C.[3] [Joseph[2] of Roseville, Shawnee County, Kansas}, Paul[1] {of Bohemia}] Kovar of

Kansas. Her mother was Edna Mae [Frank {of Ohio}, David] Lee of Kansas. Charles[3] and Mae[4] had four children: Edwin Ray[4] [adopted], Pamela Mae[4] [adopted], Brian Douglas[4] [adopted] and Bradley Duane[4] [adopted].

c. Margaret Mary[3] "Sis" Devader
born on November 12, 1922 at Emmett, Pottawatomie County, Kansas. She died on January 18, 1997 at Kansas City, Jackson County, Missouri. She married Kenneth W. Blandin on August 17, 1950 in Kansas. He was born on November 27, 1916 at Lincoln, Jackson County, Kansas. He died on June 27, 1993 at Kansas City, Jackson County, Missouri. His father was Samuel "Sam" [James Victor {who married Shay-Ah-Nah}, O. K.] Blandin, a Native American Indian born on the Prairie Band Indian Reservation at Mayetta, Jackson County, Kansas. His mother was Nora [White, Henry] Chaney of Pottawatomie County, Kansas. Margaret[3] and Kenneth had two children: Janice Darlene [adopted] and Karl Joseph [adopted].

d. Francis Joseph[3] Devader
born on January 20, 1924 at Emmett, Pottawatomie County, Kansas. He died on November 18, 1926 at Emmett, Pottawatomie County, Kansas and was buried there in the Holy Cross

Cemetery.

e. Prudence Louise[3] Devader
born on October 17, 1928 at Emmett, Pottawatomie County, Kansas. She died on October 20, 1928 at Emmett, Pottawatomie County, Kansas and was buried there in the Holy Cross Cemetery.

f. Josephine[3] Devader
born on October 4, 1929 at Emmett, Pottawatomie County, Kansas. She died on October 5, 1929 at Emmett, Pottawatomie County, Kansas and was buried there in the Holy Cross Cemetery.

g. Regina Ann[3] Devader
born on July 17, 1933 at Emmett, Pottawatomie County, Kansas. She died on January 22, 2000 in Pottawatomie County, Kansas and was buried in the Holy Cross Cemetery at Emmett. She married Galen Dean McGranahan on February 13, 1954 Wamego, Pottawatomie County, Kansas. He was born on October 10, 1929 in Kansas. He died on May 20, 1986 at Topeka, Shawnee County, Kansas and was buried in the Holy Cross Cemetery at Emmett, Pottawatomie County, Kansas. His father was George G. [Daniel Theo {of Danville, Vermilian County,

Illinois}, Abraham {of Indiana}, David] McGranahan of Warsaw, Benton County, Missouri and later of Onaga, Pottawatomie County, Kansas. His mother was Cleo B. [John J.] Bartlett of Havensville, Pottawatomie County, Kansas. Regina[3] and Galen had seven children: Laura, Theresa, John, Mary C., Rebecca, Patrick and Danny.

h. James Edwin[3] [afa Jame] Devader
born on June 2, 1935 at Emmett, Pottawatomie County, Kansas. He died of a cerebral hemmorage on July 11, 1976 at Emmett, Pottawatomie County, Kansas and was buried there in the Holy Cross Cemetery. He married Donnabelle Brewer on August 29, 1967 [another record says September 24, 1966]. She was born on March 19, 1933 at Sioux City, Woodbury County, Iowa. Her date and place of death is not known. Her father was Francis [James S. {of South Dakota}] Brewer of Illinois. Her mother was Gertrude (Unknown) of Nebraska [Editor's Note: By 1940, Francis and Gertrude were divorced]. Issue is not known.

5. Alfred John[2] Devetter/Devader
born on May 8, 1894 in Shawnee County, Kansas. He died on December 25, 1962 at Emmett, Pottawatomie County, Kansas and was buried in

the Mount Calvary Cemetery at St. Marys Pottawatomie County, Kansas. He married Emma Marie[1] Homan on April 23, 1921 [another source says April 20, 1920] in the Church of the Immaculate Conception at St. Marys, Pottawatomie County, Kansas. Emma[1] was born on April 18, 1898 at Brabander, Samara, Russia [located near Beresovka]. She died, age 59, on January 27, 1958 at St. Mary's Manor, St. Marys, Pottawatomie County, Kansas. Her father was Johan Peter[1a] "John" Homan of Brabander, Samara, Russia. Her mother was Maria Margaretha[1] "Mary" [Peter[1a], Franz[2a], Johannes[3a]] Abt of Brabander, Samara, Russia [Editor's Note: The Homans and the Abts were Volga Germans, living in Russia]. Alfred John[2] and Emma[1] had four children:

a. Rita Marie[3] Devader
born on August 28, 1924 at Emmett, Pottawatomie County, Kansas. She married Lawrence [afa Lorence] Orville[6] Thompson on April 23, 1960 in the Most Pure Heart of Mary Church at Topeka, Shawnee County, Kansas. He was born on July 3, 1921 in Kansas. He died on July 24, 2003 at Topeka, Shawnee County, Kansas. His father was John Ray[5] [Orville Burt[4] {of Burghettstown, Washington County, Pennsylvania}, David Glenn[3] {of Adams, Guernsey County,

172

Ohio}, Andrew[2] {of Alleghany County, Pennsylvania}, David[1] {of Ireland}, John[1a]] Thompson of Topeka, Shawnee County, Kansas. His mother was Gladys Glendola Fouts of Kansas. Rita[3] and Lawrence[6] had one child: Lawrence Albert Lee[7].

b. Eugene Alfred[3] Devader
born on February 7 [another researcher says the 8th], 1927 at Emmett, Pottawatomie County, Kansas. He died at birth and was buried in the Mount Calvary Cemetery at St. Marys, Pottawatomie County, Kansas.

c. Dolores Jean[3] Devader
born on January 25, 1928 at Emmett, Pottawatomie County, Kansas. During World War II, before she was married, Dolores[3] was admitted to the United States Cadet Nurse Corps on September 11, 1945 to study at the St. Francis Hospital School of Nursing where she served and studied through March 11, 1949. She married Dale Smith on October 14, 1950 in the Holy Cross Church at Emmett, Pottawatomie County, Kansas. He was born on October 15, 1927, presumably in Kansas. The name of his father and mother is not known. Dolores[3] and Dale had six children: Sandra Jean, Vicki Sue, Steven Alfred, Thomas Dale, Michael and Mary Lynn.

d. Roberta Elaine[3] Devader
born on December 5, 1929 at Emmett, Potta-
watomie County, Kansas. She married Joseph
Patrick Baumchen on February 27, 1954 in the
Immaculate Conception Church at St. Marys,
Pottawatomie County, Kansas. He was born on
March 17, 1924 at St. Marys, Pottawatomie
County, Kansas. His father was William J.
Baumchen of St. Marys, Pottawatomie County,
Kansas. His mother was Pearl (Unknown).

6. **Anna Emma[2] Devetter/Devader**
born on December 21, 1898 at Morris, Wyandotte
County, Kansas. She died on May 13, 1983 at the
residence of her daughter, Bernadine Marie
Higgins [nee Ozmer], at Annandale, Fairfax
County, Virginia and was returned for burial in
Mount Calvary Cemetery at Topeka, Shawnee
County, Kansas. She married, first, Charles Henry[3]
Trezise on November 30, 1917 at Topeka, Shawnee
County, Kansas by Ralph H. Gow, Probate Judge.
Charles[3] was born on May 24, 1893 near Emmett,
Pottawatomie County, Kansas. He died, age 25
years, 4 months and 22 days, of influenza [during
the pandemic of the Spanish Flu] on October 18,
1918 at Mesilla Park [University Park], Dona Aña
County, New Mexico and was returned home for
burial. His father was Henry P.[2] [Henry P.[1] {of St.
Just, Cornwall, England}, Henry[1a], Henry[2a]] Trezise
of England, later of Michigan, and finally of

174

Pottawatomie County, Kansas. His mother was Margaret Ellen [John {of Ohio and later of Adrian, Jackson County, Kansas}] Songs [his father's fourth wife] of Missouri City, Fort Bend County, Texas, and later of Jackson County, Kansas. Anna[2] and Charles[3] had a child: Charles Henry[4] [who died an infant of a heart condition].

Anna[2] married, second, Windsor Wilkerson "Jack" Ozmer of Fairburn, Fulton County, Georgia and later of St. Marys, Pottawatomie County, Kansas on February 8, 1921 at Kinney Heights, [a district of Kansas City], Kansas. The ceremony was performed in the Sacred Hearts Catholic Church at Kinney Heights by William DeBoeck, Rector. "Jack" was born on September 26, 1882 at Fairburn, Fulton County, Georgia. He died of acute coronary occlusion [heart attack] at 3:00 am on June 16, 1963 at Ault's Nursing Home at St. Marys, Pottawatomie County, Kansas and was buried there in the Mount Calvary Cemetery. His father was Jefferson Gadwell [Robert Clark, Richard {of Brunswick County, Virginia}, (William)] Ozmer of DeKalb County and later of Fairburn, Fulton County, Georgia. His mother was Ella Jane Hunter of Georgia. Anna Emma[2] and "Jack" had four children: Margaret Ella Leotha "Peg," Bernadine Marie Prudence "Pud," LeRoy Robert [who died as an infant] and Bernard

Francis James.

7. Henry Francis[2] Devetter/Devader
born on September 21, 1902, presumably at Morris, Wyandotte County, Kansas. He died on April 27, 1972 at Holton, Jackson County, Kansas and was buried there on April 29, 1972 in the Mount Calvary Cemetery. He married Inez Irene[3] Hladky on November 27, 1929 in Jackson County, Kansas. Inez[3] was born on October 20, 1911 [another source says, incorrectly, September 15, 1912] near Delia, Jackson County, Kansas. She died, age 93, on August 11, 2004 in the Holton Community Hospital at Holton, Jackson County, Kansas and was buried there in the Mount Calvary Cemetery. Her father was Edward E.[2] [Vaclav[1] "Joseph" {Hlatkji, a Moravian military officer of Prague, Bohemia and later a farmer of Delia, Jackson County, Kansas}] Hladky, a carpenter and farmer of St. Joseph's, Clay County, Kansas. Her mother was Albina Josephene[1] [Joseph[1a]] Macha of Moravia and later of Holy Cross, Potawatomie County, Kansas. Henry Francis[2] and Inez[3] had eight children:

a. Francis Edward[3] Devader
born on June 21, 1930 in Delia, Jackson County, Kansas. He married Edna Frances[3] Martin on March 18, 1953 in St. Patrick's Church at

Lincoln, Lancaster County, Nebraska [Editor's Note: Her brother, Ralph[3] Martin, married Reneta Bernice[3] Devader]. She was born on January 8, 1917 at Maple Hill, Wabaunsee County, Kansas. She died on November 27, 1997 at Holton, Jackson County, Kansas and was buried there in the Mount Calvary Catholic Cemetery. Her father was Henry M. [2] [Samuel L.[1] {of Germany}] Martin of Rossville, Shawnee County, Kansas. Her mother was Edith Isabel[6] [Joseph Joel Vandiver[5] {of Liberty, Crawford County, Indiana}, James Vandiver[4] {of Grant County, Kentucky}, David[3], James[2] {of Hopewell, Cumberland County, Pennsylvania}, James[1] {of Scotland}] Burns of Rossville, Shawnee County, Kansas. In 2012, Francis[3] still resided on the farm located about a mile east of Holton. Francis[3] and Edna[3] had seven children: Janice Jeane[4], Henry Francis[4], Dennis Dean[4], Peter Edward[4], Douglas Wayne[4], Lisa Diane[4] and Martin Jay[4].

Edna[3] married, first, Chester Arvil Johnson on April 28, 1941. His date and place of birth is not known. He died on May 6, 1947. His place of death is not known. Edna[3] and Chester had two children: Ingrid Marie and Daniel Eugene.

b. Robert Eugene[3] "Bob" Devader
    born on November 3, 1931 at Delia, Jackson
    County, Kansas. He married Doris Marie Van
    Manen on May 28, 1954 at Los Angeles [city of],
    California. She was born on October 11, 1934.
    Her father was Patrick Van Manen. Her mother
    was Marion (Unknown). Robert[3] and Doris
    resided in Orangevale, Sacramento County,
    California [2012]. Robert[3] and Doris had three
    children: Debbie[4], Linda[4] and Raymon[4].

c. Raymon Theodore[3] "Ted" Devader
    born on June 5, 1933 at Delia, Jackson County,
    Kansas. He died of a brain haemorrhage on
    March 17, 1992 at Holton, Jackson County,
    Kansas and was buried there in the Mt. Calvary
    Catholic Cemetery. He died just prior to retiring
    from Goodyear Tires; even so, they gave him
    his 30-year pin. He married Mary Alice Page on
    June 25, 1962 at Emmett, Pottawatomie County,
    Kansas. She was born circa 1933 near Havens-
    ville, Pottawatomie County, Kansas. Her date
    and place of death is not known. Her father was
    Charles A. [John W. {of Iowa}, William
    Shepherd {of Grayson County, Virginia}] Page
    of (near) Havensville, Pottawatomie County,
    Kansas. Her mother was Elsie May Martin of
    Highland, Doniphan County, Kansas. Ray-
    mond[3] and Mary had five children: Evonda[4],

Kimberly[4], Daymon[4] [a twin who died at birth], Raymon[4] [a twin who died at birth] and Daymon[4].

d. Ramona Mary[3] Devader
born on August 27, 1934 at Delia, Jackson County, Kansas. She married Dean Robinson on October 13, 1951 in St. Dominic's Catholic Church at Holton, Jackson County, Kansas, the Reverend Father Francis Glowaki presiding. Dean was born on October 11, 1931 in Jackson County, Kansas. His father was Johnnie Edward "John" [Samuel Jay Tilden {of Holton, Jackson County, Kansas}, James M. "Speck" {of Tennessee}] Robinson of Mayetta, Jackson County, Kansas. His mother was Bessie Leona [George Franklin, Levi W.] Ray of Mayetta, Jackson County, Kansas. In 2012 they were still farming a few acres and raising stock cattle. Prior to that, for over 50 years Dean had a bulldozing business, which his son Randy too over. Ramona[3] and Dean had three children: Vicky, Deb and Randy.

e. Richard James[3] "Dick" Devader
born on November 11, 1936 at Delia, Jackson County, Kansas. His date and place of death is not known. He married Joyce Lorraine Barton on December 29, 1956 at Holton, Jackson County, Kansas. She was born on May 15, 1942 in Jackson

County, Kansas. Her father was William "Bill" Barton of Jackson County, Kansas. Her mother was Helen (Unknown). In 2012, Richard[3] was battling leukemia; several years earlier, they had sold their cattle and they were renting out their land for hay. Richard[3] and Joyce had four children: Linda[4], Barbara[4], Thelma[4] and Cathy[4] [who died at age 9 months].

f. Renetta Bernice[3] Devader
born on February 11, 1938 at Delia, Jackson County, Kansas. She married Ralph[3] Martin in 1957 in Kansas [Editor's Note: his sister, Edna Francis[3] Martin, married Francis Edward[3] Devader]. His date and place of birth and death is not known [but died before 1973 when Renetta[3] remarried]. His father was Henry M.[2] [Samuel L.[1] {of Germany}] Martin of Rossville, Shawnee County, Kansas. His mother was Edith Isabel[6] [Joseph Joel Vandiver[5] {of Liberty, Crawford County, Indiana}, James Vandiver[4] {of Grant County, Kentucky}, David[3], James[2] {of Hopewell, Cumberland County, Pennsylvania}, James[1] {of Scotland}] Burns of Rossville, Shawnee County, Kansas. In 2012, Renetta[3] lived on her farm between Mayetta and Hoyt in Jackson County, Kansas; most of which had been sold off years earlier. Renetta[3] and Ralph had three children: Bill, Rusty and Jackie.

Renetta[3] married, second, Harold Moore in 1973. His date and place of birth and death is not known. Renetta[3] and Harold had a child: Jennie.

g. Rosealee Marie[3] Devader
born on April 29, 1939 at Delia, Jackson County, Kansas. She married Delbert Boling on December 21, 1963. He was born on May 28, 1938 in Kansas. His father was Gilbert Lemoine [Charles Lemoine {of Ohio}, George W. {of Virginia}] Boling of St. Clere, Pottawatomie County, Kansas. His mother was Arvilla Marie Patterson of Topeka, Shawnee County, Kansas. In 2012, Delbert, who was retired from Goodyear, and Rosealee[3] were living on their farm near Hoyt, Jackson County, Kansas. Rosealee[3] and Delbert had two children: Scott and Michelle.

h. Roger Forrest[3] Devader
born on November 24, 1947 in Jackson County, Kansas. He married Sarah Strawn on September 16, 1966 at Denison, Jackson County, Kansas. She was born on May 24, 1947 in either Jefferson County or Jackson County, Kansas. Her father was William Ellis[8] [John William[7], John Hughes[6] {of Waynesburg, Greene County, Pennsylvania}, Samuel[5], Isaiah[4] {of Haycock, Bucks County, Pennsylvania}, Jacob[3] {of Bethlehem, Hunterdon County, New Jersey}, Jaccob[2] {of Middletown,

Bucks County, Pennsylvania}, Lancelot[1] {Staughan of Kincardineshire, Fife County, Scotland}, Alexander[1a] {Strachan}, Alexander[2a], Alexander Glas[3a] {of Lucas, Edinburgh, Scotland}] Strawn of Valley Falls, Jefferson County, Kansas. Her mother was Harriet Agnes[11] {afa Adaline} [William Ovid[10] {of Bolter, Humboldt County, Iowa}, Ransom Henry[9] {of Medina, Medina County, Ohio}, Elijah Henry[8] {of Blandford, Hampden County, Massachusetts}, Ransom[7], Levi[6] {Guile of Preston, New London County, Connecticut}, John[5], John[4], Samuel[3] {of Haverhill, Essex County, Massachusetts}, John[2], Samuel[1] {of Ilketshall, Wangford, Suffolk, England}, Richard[1a] {Gyle of Westhall, Dunwich, Suffolk, England}, Richard[2a], Will[3a] {born circa 1520)] Gile of Lincoln, Republic County, Kansas. In 2012 they were living several miles north of Mayetta, Jackson County, Kansas on Roger[3]'s parents farm where they raised an Australian breed of sheep. Roger[3] and Sarah also owned a gift shop in Holton. Roger[3] and Sarah had a child: Matt[4].

Marriage License for
Peter Devader & Prudanse Cousman

Tombstone of
Peter Devader and Prudanse Cousman

The Life and Times of
Jacobus-Francies[1a] D'Huyvettere

PATERNAL ANCESTRY: [DEVETTER/
DUIVETTER/D'HUYVETTERE: (Unknown)]

MATERNAL ANCESTRY: [(Unknown)]

JACOBUS-FRANCIES[1a] was born circa 1828 at Water-vliet, Oost-Vlaanderen, Flanders, Belgium. He died sometime before 1885 [when his wife and children migrated to America] at Watervliet, Oost-Vlaanderen, Flanders, Belgium.. The name of his father and mother is not known.

JACOBUS-FRANCIES[1a] married Josephine Seraphina[1a] "Finia" DeSmet. The date of their marriage [sometime before 1860, when their first child was born], presumably at Watervliet, Oost-Vlaanderen, Flanders, Belgium, is not known. Seraphina[1a] was born on May 10, 1832 at Watervliet, Oost-Vlaanderen, Flanders. She died on Ascension Day, May 21, 1914, at Convent, Bassevelde, Belgium. Her father was Jacobus Bernardus[2a] [Peter Judocus[3a]] DeSmet of Watervliet, Oost-Vlaanderen, Flanders, Belgium. Her mother was Sophie[2a] Heetezone of Watervliet, Oost-Vlaanderen, Flanders, Belgium.

Seraphina[1a] came to America in 1835 with her five children, arriving first in New York City, then went to Paterson, Passaic County, New Jersey, then to Pittsburgh, Pennsylvania. Eventually, they settled in the area of Molina, Rock Island County, Illinois where her brother Pieter lived in a Belgian settlement there.

Seraphina[1a] was soon found living with her sister Matilda[1a], who never married, in the area of Annawan, Henry County, Illinois. After Matilda[1a] died at the early age of 29, Seraphina[1a] returned to Belgium, where she later died. There is a family story that Matilda[1a] was engaged to a young man in the army. They were planning to be married when his tour was up; however, he was killed and she died of a broken heart.

JACOBUS-FRANCIES[1a] was a farmer, raised cattle and, at one time, is believed to have been the proprietor of a tavern.

The Children of
Jacobus-Francies[1a] D'Huyvettere
and Josephine Seraphina[1a] DeSmet

1. **Peter Edward[1] D'Huyvettere/Duivetter**
   born on February 22, 1860 at Watervliet, Oost-Vlaanderen, Flanders, Belgium. He died on March 16, 1929 at Emmett, Pottowatomie County, Kansas and was buried there in the Holy Cross Cemetery. He married Prudanse Sophie[1] Cousman [also found as Coesman and Coesmant] on October 19, 1885 in a Catholic Church at Atkinson, Henry County, Illinois. Prudanse[1] was born on June 7, 1863 at St. Lauriens, Flanders, Belgium. She died on June 28, 1914 at Emmett, Pottowatomie County, Kansas and was buried there in the Holy Cross Cemetery. Her father was Joseph E.[1a] Cousman of St. Lauriens, Flanders, Belgium. Her mother was Marie Therese[1a] [Anthony[2a]] DeVos of St. Lauriens, Flanders, Belgium. Peter[1] and Prudanse[1] had seven children: Mary Josephine[2] "Louise," Edward Joseph[2], John Thomas[2], Charles E.[2], Alfred John[2], Anna Emma[2] and Henry Francis[2].

2. **Edward[1] D'Huyvettere/Duvetter**
   born in January 1862 at Watervliet, Oost-Vlaanderen, Flanders, Belgium. He died in 1936 at Moline, Rock Island County, Illinois. He married Anna[1] (Unknown) sometime before 1905 [when their first

child was born], presumably in Rock Island County, Illinois. She was born circa 1886 in Sweden. She died sometime between 1910 [when she last appears on the U. S. Census] and 1920, presumably in Rock Island County, Illinois. Edward[1] arrived in the USA on May 2, 1881 at New York and was naturalized a citizen on March 1, 1889. Edward[1] and Anna[1] had two children:

a. Raymond C.[2] Devetter
born circa 1905 in Rock Island County, Illinois. His date of death, presumably at Fort Madison, Lee County, Iowa, is not known. He only completed the fifth grade.

b. Henry C.[2] Devetter
born circa 1906 in Rock Island County, Illinois. His date of death, presumably at Fort Madison, Lee County, Iowa, is not known. He only completed the fifth grade.

[Editor's Note: Both Raymond[2] and Henry[2], along with an accomplice named Lester Joe McCrossen were arrested and subsequently imprisoned for life in the Iowa State Penitentiary at Fort Madison, Lee County, Iowa for kidnapping and assaulting two girls]

3. Emil/Emiel[1] "Mel" D'Huyvettere/Devetter
born on February 22, 1864 at Watervliet, Oost-Vlaanderen, Flanders, Belgium. He died on July 1, 1934 at Atkinson, Henry County, Illinois and was buried there in the St. Anthony's Catholic Church Cemetery. He married Mary Louise[2] Dollander in 1887 in St. Anthony's Church at Atkinson, Henry County, Illinois. She was born in 1869 at Atkinson, Henry County, Illinois and later baptized there at the St. Anthony's Catholic Church. She died, age 29, in 1898 at Atkinson, Henry County, Illinois and was buried there in the St. Anthony's Catholic Church Cemetery [Editor's Note: Their daughter, Mary[2], was nine at the time and she quit school and kept house and took care of her younger siblings]. Mary[2] Dollander's father was Leopold[1] Dollander of Watervliet, Oost Vlaanderern, Flanders, Belgium. Her mother was Rosalie O.[1] Osterlink of Watervliet, Oost Vlaanderen, Flanders, Belgium. Emil[1] and Mary[2] had six children:

a. Mary Madeline[2] "Maud" Devader
born on November 10, 1888 at Atkinson, Henry County, Illinois. She died in March 1970 at Woonsocket, Sanborn County, South Dakota. She married Johanas [afa John] Bernard[2] "Jack" Vermeulen on May 12, 1908 at Annawan, Henry County, Illinois. He was born on September 10, 1884 at Atkinson, Henry County, Illinois. He died

on June 22, 1950 in Sanborn County, South
Dakota. His father was Evo[1] Vermeulen of
Belgium. His mother was Mary M.[1] Buysse of
Belgium. Mary[2] and John[2] had seven children:
Theresa Madeline[3], Raphael Francis[3], Sylvia
Marie[3], Margaret Elizabeth[3], Bernard Evo[3],
Robert Edward[3] [who died at birth] and Donald
Eugene[3].

b. Amelia[2] "Nellie" Devader
born on December 29, 1891 in Henry County,
Illinois. She died on December 30, 1991, probably
in Henry County, Illinois. She married Eilert Ben[3]
Miller on February 6, 1912 in the Peoria Court
House at Peoria, Peoria County, Illinois [Editor's
Note: While the rest of the family was Catholic,
"Nellie" belonged to the United Methodist
Church at Annawan]. He was born on June 29,
1888 at Washington, Tazwell County [another
record says Peoria Court House, Peoria County],
Illinois. He died on December 28, 1969 [another
researcher says May 18th] at Annawan, Henry
County, Illinois and was buried there in the
Annawan Cemetery. His father was Albert J.[2]
[John C.[1] {of Germany}] Miller of Washington,
Tazwell County, Illinois. His mother was Mary
Catherine[2] "Marie" [Eilet H.[1] {of Germany}]
Harms of Linn, Woodford County, Illinois.
Amelia[2] and Eilert[3] had two children: Richard[4]

and Hazel[4].

c. Frank[2] Devader
    born in 1893 at Annawan, Henry County, Illinois.
    He died in 1895 at Annawan, Henry County,
    Illinois.

d. Matilda[2] Devader
    born on January 25, 1895 at Annawan, Henry
    County, Illinois. She died on March 29, 1972 at
    Annawan, Henry County, Illinois. She married
    Mandus [afa Amandre] Francis[3] VanDer Snick on
    December 21, 1916 at Annawan, Henry County,
    Illinois. He was born on December 21, 1891 in
    Illinois. He died on March 15, 1954 in Illinois.
    His father was Michael[2] [Amandus[1] {of Bearlear,
    Belgium}] VanDerSnick of Chicago, Cook
    County, Illinois. His mother was Louise[2]
    [Leopold[1] {of Antwerp, Belgium}] Doubler of
    Atkinson, Henry County, Illinois. Matilda[2] and
    Mandus[3] had four children: Walter M.[4], Michael
    M.[4], Marilyn[4] and Catherine[4].

e. Bertha Marie[2] Devader
    born on January 25, 1897 at Annawan, Henry
    County, Illinois. She died on November 28, 1975
    in Illinois. She married Jay Johnson[2] Poulter on
    December 15, 1915 at Kewanee, Henry County,
    Illinois. He was born on July 4, 1892 at Rock Falls,

Whiteside County, Illinois. He died on December 24, 1949 at Rock Falls, Whiteside County, Illinois. His father was John[1] Poulter of Yorkshire, England and later of Rock Falls, Whiteside County, Illinois. His mother was Fannie[1] [Ralph[1a]] Johnson of Yorkshire, England and later of Rock Falls, Whiteside County, Illinois. Bertha[2] and Jay[2] had four children: Emil[3], Irene[3], Vicki[3] and Kathryn[3].

f. Robert Edward[2] Devader
born in 1899 in Henry County, Illinois. He died in February 1969 at Green Bay, Brown County, Wisconsin and was buried there in the Fort Howard Cemetery. He married McClaire "Clara" LaPlant. She died in 1920 [shortly after her daughter Virginia was born] and was buried there in the Holy Cross Cemetery at Green Bay, Brown County, Wisconsin. Robert Edward[2] and McClaire had two children: Virginia[3] and David John[3] [Editor's Note: After their mother died, their father was unable to care for them himself and couldn't find family to help him, so the children spent a number of years at the Guardian Angles Boarding School in Oneida County, Wisconsin].

4. Julius J.[1] D'Huyvettere/Devetter
born on March 1, 1866 at Watervliet, Oost-Vlaan-deren, Flanders, Belgium. He died on February 28, 1938 in the Swenson Memorial Hospital at Canby, Yellow Medicine County, Minnesota and was buried in the St. Eloi Cemetery at Ghent, Lyon County, Minnesota. He married, first, Lovisia[1] "Louise" Maynard on April 24, 1890 in Henry County, Illinois. She was born on December 25, 1869 at Brabant Wallon, Belgium [Editor's Note: She arrived in America in 1876 at age 7]. She died on September 29, 1921. Her place of death is not known, but possibly Westerheim, Lyon County, Minnesota. The name of her father is not known. Her mother was Rosalie (Unknown). [Editor's Note: Louise may have either been married first to another unknown person or had a child by him, producing a son named Charles; family members believe she gave Charles to her parents to raise.] Julius[1] came to the United States in 1880, at age 14, and is said to have settled near Pattersonville, New Jersey [Editor's Note: probably East Patterson, Bergen County, New Jersey]. He later moved to the Rock Island, Rock Island County, Illinois area where for 25 years he farmed near Tracy, Lyon County, Minnesota. It is not clear if they moved to Ghent, Lyon County, Minnesota while "Louise" was still alive. Julius[1] and Lovisia[1] had eight children:

a. Alphonse Edward[2] Devader
born on June 14, 1891 in Illinois. He died on July 17, 1954 in Lyon County, Minnesota. He married Emilie Paulina[2] Illian on February 18, 1914 at Tracy, Lyon County, Minnesota. She was born on February 1, 1894 in Plymouth County, Iowa. She died on March 14, 1960 in Lyon County, Minnesota. Her father was Charles Adam[1] [Frederick William[1a]} Illian of Bad Pyrmont, Hamlen-Pyrmont, Niedersachsen, Germany and later of Lyon County, Minnesota. Her mother was Emelie H.[1] [Joachim[1a]] Knaack of Prussia and later of Lyon County, Minnesota. Alphonse[2] was in the trucking business, transporting natural ice. Alphonse[2] and Emilie[2] had five children; Lillian Mildren[3], Gerald Gordon[3], Eunice Marie[3], Arlene[3] and Joan[3].

Julius, Lovisia and
Alphonse (child)

b. Edmond H.[2] Devader
born on April 28, 1894 in Illinois. His date and place of death is not known. He lived at Westorheim, Lyon County and Wilmar, Kandiyohi County, Minnesota. He never married and lived as a hermit all of his life.

c. Lillian Mildred[2] [afa Nellie] Devader
born on June 12, 1897 in Illinois. She died on November 18, 1983 at West Chester, Chester County, Pennsylvania. She married Leo Joseph[2] Buysse on January 30, 1917 in the St. Edwards Church in Minnesota. He was born on July 23, 1892 in Minnesota. He died on November 9, 1964 in Yellow Medicine County, Minnesota. His father was Frank[1] Buysse of St. Margurita, East Flanders, Belgium and later of Lyon County, Minnesota. His mother was Leonore[1] Wambeke of Belgium and later of Minnesota. Lilian[2] and Leo[2] had eight children: Raymond Leo[3], Walter Clarence[3], John Lou[3], Lester Louis[3], James Eugene[3], Rita[3], Francis Joseph[3] and Norma Jean[3].

d. Alice[2] Devader
date of birth in Illinois is unknown. She died an infant.

e. Julius J.[2] Devader, Jr.
date of birth in Illinois is unknown. He died an
infant.

f. Victor A.[2] Devader
date and place of birth is not known. His date of
death in Colorado is not known. He was a nomad
who, according to the family, in his late fifties
finally married. Nothing else is known of him.

g. Raymond Clarence[2] Devader
born in 1906 in Illinois [but possibly Minnesota].
He died in 1962, presumably in Codington
County, South Dakota. He married Bernice M.[3]
Torgerson on May 17, 1930 at Watertown,
Codington County, South Dakota. She was born
on September 8, 1905 at Riverside, Luc Qu Parle
County, Minnesota. She died in March 1979, at
Watertown, Luc Qu Parle County, Minnesota.
Her father was Forger C.[2] [John[1] {of Norway}]
Torgerson of Luc Qu Parle County, Minnesota.
Her mother was Gustav Irine (Unknown) of Luc
Qu Parle County, Minnesota. Raymond[2] was a
fireman at Watertown, Codington County, South
Dakota. Raymond[2] and Bernice had three
children: Tracy[3], Allison[3] and Eric[3].

h. Florian Lawrence[2] Devader
born on June 18, 1908 in Lyon County, Minnesota. He died on January 29, 1981 at Tracy, Lyon County, Minnesota. He married Mabel Winnifred[2] Hallett on September 17, 1935 at Tracy, Lyon County, Minnesota. She was born on January 8, 1908 at Tracy, Lyon County, Minnesota. She died on November 21, 2000 at Tracy, Lyon County, Minnesota. Her father was Charles[1] Hallett of England. Her mother was Hannah[1] (Unknown) of England. Florian[2] was a landscaper. Florian[2] and Mabel[2] had six children: Charles Dale[3], David[3], Virginia Marie[3], Patricia[3], Donna[3] and Kathleen Louise[3].

Julius[1] married, second, Prudence[1] Van Huffell in November 1926 in Minnesota. Prudence[1] was born circa 1886 at Watervliet, Oost-Vlaanderen, Flanders, Belgium. She died on August 3, 1933, probably in Yellow Medicine County, Minnesota. The name of her father and mother is not known. There was no issue from this marriage.

Julius[1] married, third, Leona[1] Clarys on October 31, 1934, probably in Yellow Medicine County, Minnesota. She was born circa 1886 at Watervliet, Oost-Vlaanderen, Flanders, Belgium. Her date and place of death is not known. The name of her father and mother is not known. There was no issue from this marriage.

5. Mathilde[1] "Tillie" D'Huyvettere/Duvetter
born on April 10, 1869 at Watervliet, Oost-Vlaanderen, Flanders, Belgium [another record says she
was born in March 1871 at Brabant, Wallon,
Flanders, Belgium]. She died on May 26, 1902 at
Moline, Rock Island County, Illinois. She never
married.

[EDITOR'S NOTE: Some researchers list a sixth child]

6. Bruno D'Huyvettere
date of birth at Watervliet, Oost-Vlaanderen, Flanders, Belgium is not known. His date and place of
death is not known [apparently he died young].

ADDENDA PAGE

Pg Ref #   Comment/Correction/Addition/Etc.

_____

_____

_____

_____

_____

_____

_____

_____

_____

_____

_____

_____

_____

_____

_____

_____